Neural Networks for Financial Forecasting

Neural Networks for Financial Forecasting

Edward Gately
Series Editor: Perry J. Kaufman

John Wiley & Sons, Inc.
New York • Chichester • Brisbane • Toronto • Singapore

Copyright © 1996 by Edward J. Gately
Published by John Wiley & Sons, Inc.

Library of Congress Cataloging-in-Publication Data:

Gately, Ed, 1929–
     Neural networks for financial forecasting / Ed Gately.
          p.   cm. — (Wiley trader's advantage series)
     Includes bibliographical references and index.
     ISBN 0-471-11212-7 (acid-free paper)
     1. Program trading (Securities)   2. Neural networks (Computer
science)   I. Title.   II. Series.
     HG4515.5.G37   1996
     332.6' 0285—dc20   95-8998

Printed in the United States of America
10   9   8   7   6   5   4   3   2   1

To Susan Lynn Gately and Louise Marie Gately
The loves of my life, and Robyn Gately—long may
his spirit live.

THE TRADER'S ADVANTAGE SERIES PREFACE

The Trader's Advantage Series is a new concept in publishing for traders and analysts of futures, options, equity, and generally all world economic markets. Books in the series present single ideas with only that background information needed to understand the content. No long introductions, no definitions of the futures contract, clearing house, and order entry. Focused.

The futures and options industry is no longer in its infancy. From its role as an agricultural vehicle it has become the alterego of the most active world markets. The use of EFPs (exchange for physicals) in currency markets makes the selection of physical or futures markets transparent, in the same way the futures markets evolved into the official pricing vehicle for world grain. With a single telephone call, a trader or investment manager can hedge a stock portfolio, set a crossrate, perform a swap, or buy the protection of an inflation index. The classic regimes can no longer be clearly separated.

And this is just the beginning. Automated exchanges are penetrating traditional open outcry markets. Even now, from the time the transaction is completed in the pit, everything else is electronic. "Program trading" is the automated response to the analysis of a computerized ticker tape, and it is just the tip of the inevitable evolutionary process. Soon the executions will be computerized and then we won't be able to call anyone to complain about a fill. Perhaps we won't even have to place an order to get a fill.

Market literature has also evolved. Many of the books written on trading are introductory. Even those intended for more advanced audiences often include a review of contract specifications and market mechanics. There are very few books specifically targeted for the experienced and professional traders and analysts. *The Trader's Advantage Series* changes all that.

This series presents contributions by established professionals and exceptional research analysts. The authors' highly specialized talents have been applied primarily to futures, cash, and equity markets but are often generally applicable to price forecasting. Topics in the series will include trading systems and individual techniques, but all are a necessary part of the development process that is intrinsic to improving price forecasting and trading.

These works are creative, often state-of-the-art. They offer new techniques, in-depth analysis of current trading methods, or innovative and enlightening ways of looking at still unsolved problems. The ideas are explained in a clear, straightforward manner with frequent examples and illustrations. Because they do not contain unnecessary background material they are short and to the point. They require careful reading, study, and consideration. In exchange, they contribute knowledge to help build an unparalleled understanding of all areas of market analysis and forecasting.

NEURAL NETWORKS FOR FINANCIAL FORECASTING

This book will teach you how to use neural networks to create financial trading strategies. It is a clear, step-by-step approach to neural network applications—the only one I have seen so far. Ed Gately has done us all a great service by sharing his own experiences using the most important and powerful analytic tool to arrive in the past fifteen years (which is a long time considering the advances in computer technology).

Neural nets are an incredibly flexible tool. This technique enhances your ability to integrate fundamental and technical data. It is rapidly replacing traditional econometrics methods while its resources still remain mostly untapped. It can uncover cause-and-effect relationships and isolates subtle patterns that cannot be found using other tools.

It is especially interesting that this method does not need continuous relationships between the data that is being evaluated in order to identify key events or patterns. Traditional analysis, for example, requires that the tradeoffs between supply and demand, economic growth, and interest rates, always be treated with the same importance over the long term. They must conform to a rigid formula. Neural nets are much more adaptable and can come closer to reality by applying one set of interactive data now, and a completely different group when circumstances change.

But this tremendous power holds as much danger as it does potential. Patterns can be found where none exist. The ability to compare interrelationships during isolated time intervals allows the program to find many coincidental patterns, having nothing to do with the problem. It is necessary for the user to control this process. You must limit the inputs to those that make sense, avoid duplication, and verify that the solution works. It is not the tool that fails, it is the one who uses it.

Ed Gately follows one primary example throughout the book. He goes, step-by-step through input selection, network specification, evaluation of results, and how to decide when you are done. It is important that the beginning be learned properly; it will prevent future problems. I hope you enjoy this book and find it as valuable as I have.

PERRY KAUFMAN

Wells River, Vermont

PREFACE

The rapid creation of new neural network architectures and training algorithms combined with the rapid increase in power of personal computers has lead to the development of much more robust neural networks for financial forecasting.

Many of the neural software packages that are sold today end up on a shelf somewhere because the promised results are not delivered. This book will help those new to using neural networks reach the results he or she is seeking.

My conversations at seminars have indicated that beginners often fall into the classic traps of not maintaining data integrity and using data that is nontypical, such as including market action data accumulated during the Persian Gulf War. These common mistakes are not covered in any other neural text with which I am acquainted.

Most neural network books can be classified as either academic or introductory. The beginning texts do not address the matters of classic errors or the need for testing of inputs, architectures, and training algorithms; the academic texts address these concerns, but tend to be top heavy on mathematics. It is my intention to provide a book that bridges the gap between these two approaches.

ED GATELY

Mahwah, New Jersey

ACKNOWLEDGMENTS

I wish to thank the following people who have contributed directly and indirectly to the writing of this book.

John P. Glass and David Hafler who have been my mentors during most of my adult life.

Steve Ward of Ward Systems who encouraged my efforts in innumerable ways and opened my eyes to what could be accomplished using neural networks.

Tim Slater of CompuTrac who encouraged my early efforts with neural networks.

Perry Kaufman whose command of the English language has contributed greatly to the readability of this book and whose encouragement has been greatly appreciated.

Jaqueline Urinyi, my editor at John Wiley & Sons.

Randall B. Caldwell of *NeuroVe$t Journal*.

Anita Greiter for her word processing skills.

CONTENTS

Neural Networks for Financial Forecasting

1

BIOLOGICAL BRAIN AND ARTIFICIAL NEURAL NETWORKS (ANN)

In this chapter, both the macro and micro structure of the brain will be presented. A brief history of mechanical analog and digital computing is followed by a history of artificial neural networks. The structure of artificial neural networks is introduced, and compared to biological neural networks. Suitable and unsuitable problems for artificial networks are examined.

MACRO BRAIN STRUCTURE

All living things have brains composed of cells called *neurons*. These cells are unique in that they do not die, unlike the other cells in an organism. This may account for the fact that we can remember things that took place decades ago. Estimates of the number of neurons in the human brain go as high as 100 billion. Even the lowly slug has 20,000 neurons.

The human brain is divided vertically into two approximately equal-sized parts. Each "half" serves very different and complementary roles in human activity (Figure 1–1). Studies show that the left side of the brain is devoted to the logical and mathematical functions, while the right side of the brain deals with the emotions, pattern

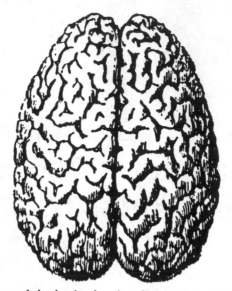

Figure 1-1   Top view of the brain showing division into left and right halves.

recognition, and the intuitive senses. Although all people use both sides of the brain, in most people one of the sides is dominant. Scientists and mathematicians are said to be left-brain people. Artists and writers are said to be right-brain people. The book *Drawing On the Right Side of the Brain* is directed at artists to assist them in getting more in touch with sensitivity, reactions, and abstraction. In the financial world, fundamental and technical analysis is left-brain oriented because it relies on mathematical operations. On the other hand, neural networks act as if they are right-side oriented, because they rely on hidden relationships between inputs and pattern recognition to make their forecasts.

BACKGROUND ON MECHANICAL-ELECTRONIC ANALOG AND DIGITAL COMPUTING

Much work has been done to develop mechanical and electronic devices to mimic the brain's abilities in order to reduce the amount of effort required to solve intellectual problems. Crude mechanical adding machines had been developed by the late 1700s. During the 1930s, scientists at Bell Laboratories were developing electronic analog computers that not only did the four basic mathematical operations, but also performed the advanced functions of differentiation and integration. One of the important applications of this work was the inertial-guidance systems that directed airplanes and missiles across oceans with errors measured in fractions of a mile.

THE DEVELOPMENT OF ARTIFICIAL NEURAL NETWORKS

By the 1940s, sophisticated mechanical devices had been developed that added, subtracted, multiplied, and divided. The *ultimate* machine, the envy of every accountant and engineer of the 1950s, was the Frieden desk-top calculator, which not only did the basic four functions, but also calculated square roots with the pressing of one key.

During the same period, scientists at the University of Pennsylvania were developing the first digital computer. This very crude computer was named ENIAC. ENIAC became the father of "mainframe" computers of immense power. All of this development was intended to mimic the functions done by the left side of the brain.

In 1943 Warren McCullock and Walter Pitts published a paper entitled "A Logical Calculus of Ideas Immanent in Nervous Activity" (*Bulletin of Mathematical Biophysics,* Volume 5, pp. 115–133). This paper laid the theoretical basis for the subsequent development of current artificial neural networks. In 1951, MIT student Marvin Minsky built a neural computer and set it up to solve the problem of learning a maze. This was the beginning of the field of Artificial Intelligence, and Dr. Minsky, who is still at MIT, is often referred to as the father of expert systems.

In the late 1970s, computers had been developed with sufficient power to begin practical research on artificial neural networks or ANN. However, it was the development of back-propagation in 1986 that enabled neural networks to solve everyday business, scientific, and industrial problems.

An artificial neural network or ANN is a software program that mimics the human brain's ability to classify patterns or to make predictions or decisions based on past experience. The human brain relies on inputs from the five senses, while the artificial neural network uses inputs from data sets.

Because practical neural networks have been available only since the 1970s and because their development has been dependent on computer power, among other things, neural network development is still in its infancy. The speed of solving the problem and the use of neural networks is dependent on the size of the network, as exemplified by the complexity of the problem and the number of examples presented to the network as well as the speed of the computer. Faster computers mean either bigger problems solved in the same time or the same size problems solved in less time. The difference between a 286 computer (8 or 12 mHz) and a 486DX33 computer is roughly eight to one in processing power. The new Pentium-90 quadruples that speed. The new processing chips on the drawing boards promise to again double that performance. These chips may well be 32 times as fast as the 286 chip—all before the turn of the century.

APPLICATIONS OF NEURAL NETWORKS

Neural Networks have been applied to many real-world situations, among them medical diagnostics, product inspection, oilwell exploration, speech recognition, flight control, terrain classification, coin grading, river flood stage prediction, machine tool controls, race track betting, and financial forecasting. Financial areas where neural networks have found extensive applications include:

Credit card fraud	Option pricing
Bankruptcy prediction	Sales prospect selection
Credit card applications	Capital markets analysis
Mortgage applications	Managerial decision making
Product marketing	Travel voucher screening
Corporate bond grading	Security risk profiling
Municipal bond grading	Economic indicator forecasts
Stock market prediction	Property tax analysis
Bank failure prediction	Cash flow forecasting
Stock selection	Locating of tax evaders
Currency price prediction	Mutual fund selection
Real estate appraisal	Predicting changes in market trend
Crop forecasting	
Commodity trading	Forecasting personnel requirements
Arbitrage pricing	
Analysis of corporate financial health	Forecasting machine tool loading

MICRO BRAIN STRUCTURE

As mentioned earlier, biological brains are composed of cells called *neurons*. Each neuron (Figure 1–2) has a cell body or soma, from which extends a single axon, along which impulses are transmitted to other neurons when the soma is sufficiently excited by incoming impulses. These incoming impulses are received by sensors called *dendrites*. The area where the impulses are received is called a *synapse*. Nerve impulses are transmitted from one neuron to another across *synapses*. These neural structures operate electrochemically. This means that the brain works on electrical impulses that are created by chemical actions. When the combined interplay of many incoming impulses reaches a level of excitement or electrical charge called a threshold, the soma releases its charge (depolarizes), and sends a nerve action potential down its axon to other nerve cells and their dendrites. The transmission of nerve impulses across a synaptic gap involves the release of chemical transmitters called biogenic amines, formed from amino acids.

Schematically, the neuron can be represented as a cell having a number of inputs and an output which is interconnected to other neurons (see Figure 1–3). Thus when a neuron depolarizes and sends a nerve action potential down its axon, it is sending this signal to many more neurons.

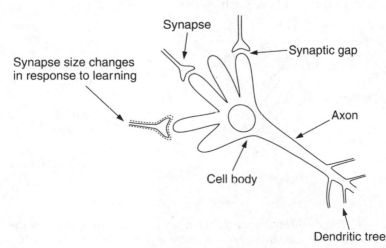

Figure 1–2   Details of a biological neuron.

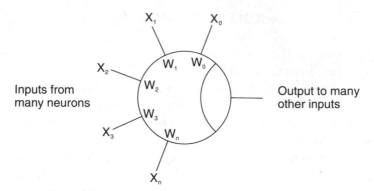

Figure 1–3 Schematic representation of a biological neuron showing how the neuron combines many inputs into an output that is in turn connected to many other neurons. For clarity, only one of many outputs is shown. The Xs represent inputs and the Ws are the interconnections between the inputs.

In computers, artificial neural networks appear very similar to the schematic of a human brain. Compare Figure 1–3 to Figure 1–4. The effect of the biological synaptic gap is analogous in artificial neural networks to the weight or measure of importance of the interconnections between the artificial neurons. The nonlinear characteristics of brain neurons is modeled in ANNs by using nonlinear connections between the neurons.

Artificial neural networks have three or more layers of neurons. The first layer of neurons, called the *input layer,* has one neuron for each input to the network. Each neuron in the input layer is connected

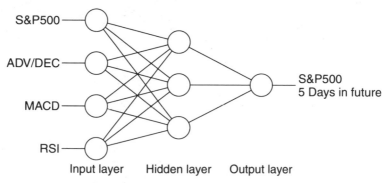

Figure 1–4 Simple three-layer artificial neural network for predicting the S&P 500 five days in advance using today's value of the S&P, the Advance/Decline Index, MACD, and RSI as inputs.

to every neuron in a hidden area. The hidden area occasionally consists of more than one layer, in which case each neuron in the first hidden layer will be connected to every neuron in the second hidden layer. If the hidden layer consists of more than two hidden layers, the neurons in the second hidden layer will be connected to every neuron in the third hidden layer. The last layer of the hidden area is connected to the *outer* layer. Figure 1–4 illustrates a simple 3-layer network (input, hidden, and output layers) where every neuron in the input layer is connected to every neuron in the hidden layer, and the neurons in the hidden layer are similarly connected to the neuron in the output layer.

The *strength* of the connection between the various neurons varies with the purpose of the network. It is the strength of the connection between neurons that makes two otherwise identical networks different. The strength of the connection between two neurons is referred to as *weight*. A strong connection has greater weight than a weaker connection. Important inputs are given large weighting values. The biological brain filters unimportant information by discarding it. This is the same as giving it a weight (importance) of zero.

Perhaps the most important difference between natural neural networks (the brain) and artificial neural networks is that the inputs to the brain come from the five senses. In the case of artificial or computer neural networks, the inputs are numbers and anything we want to use as an input to an artificial neural network must be converted to a number (digitized). In many applications, artificial neural networks use just the numbers 0 and +1, to indicate that the input is either present or not present. Surprisingly, this does not reduce the ability of the network to find a good solution.

SUITABLE PROBLEMS FOR THE ARTIFICIAL NEURAL NETWORK

Much as the human brain can learn to solve many problems, so can the artificial neural network learn to solve certain problems. The learning process is very similar; it involves the repeated exposure to the material to be learned and reinforcement of the correct answer.

The brain has no difficulty solving the arithmetic problem $2.000 + 2.000 = 4.000$. Nor does it have a problem distinguishing between an apple and a flower. The artificial neural network (which we will call neural network or ANN from here forward) has great difficulty solving the 2.000 + 2.000 problem *exactly*. Sometimes it will get the answer 3.933 and other times 4.008. Because the ANN process is intuitive rather than rational, it will get the *exact* answer 4.000 only rarely. These types of mathematical problems are best solved by using conventional calculators and computers.

However, the neural network would have *no* problem recognizing the difference between the apple and the flower. They are both round, and the apple has a smooth, relatively hard surface, while the flower has petals and a surface that is relatively soft.

In Chapter 2, we will present an overview of artificial neural networks including the steps necessary to build, train and use an artificial neural network.

2

OVERVIEW OF ARTIFICIAL NEURAL NETWORKS

COMPARING NEURAL NETS TO THE HUMAN BRAIN

An *artificial* neural network is a computer software program that mimics the human brain's ability to classify patterns or to make forecasts or decisions based on past experience. The human brain relies on neural stimuli while the neural network uses mathematical data sets or vectors, which take the form of specific lists of information.

Artificial neural networks differ from the human brain in several ways. They do not get bored, take coffee breaks, want to be paid, take holidays or vacations; they just keep chugging along. Their capacity is very small, a few hundred neurons, versus the billions of neurons in the human brain. This size can be attributed to the limits of the current level of technology and computer speed. The smallness means that if they are to be successful, they must be very specialized. This specialization is what keeps them focused on the task at hand. This limitation has another advantage. It can prevent a neural network solution from becoming too specific, or to "overfit" a solution. Therefore this limitation produces a faster, more meaningful and more general answer.

Another difference is that computer neural networks work only with numbers, while the human brain gets simultaneous input from

9

Factor	Brain	Neural Network
Size	Very large, up to 100 billion neurons	Relatively small, rarely more than a few hundred neurons
Inputs	5 senses	Data sets, reduced to numbers, (digitized)
Work ethic	Good, but easily bored and often unfocused	Mechanical, solves only what is asked
Specialization	Yes, but with many interests and skills; can be easily distracted	1 task only
Construction	Biological	Mathematical
Interconnections per neuron	Up to 1000 not uncommon	Limited by state of art, rarely as many as 100
Brain side	Two, left and right (Analytic and intuitive)	Right side, only (intuitive)

Figure 2–1   Differences between human brain and neural network.

the five senses. The interconnection of the neurons in the computer network is much more limited than in the case of the neurons in the human brain. A biological neuron in the brain is interconnected to a thousand or more other neurons, while an simulated neuron in a neural network is limited to connecting the number of hidden neurons incorporated in the network. This is rarely as many as one hundred, and usually closer to 10. These differences have been itemized in Figure 2–1.

The training and use of an artificial neural network requires following a discrete set of steps. Each is important for determining the degree of success of the effort. These steps will be discussed in extensive detail in later chapters; however, an overview of these steps is provided here.

- *Step 1. Determine What Is to Be Forecast.* Forecasting the snowfall in Vermont in November, while of some business interest, is irrelevant to your trading of the S&P 500.

- *Step 2. Collect Data Sets or Number Series That Have a Relationship to What Is to Be Forecast.* This information will be used to create the forecast. Your golf score on Sunday will have little relationship to the price of the S&P 500 a week from now, however, today's price of oil may have a large effect on next weeks S&P 500 price.

- *Step 3. Preprocess the Data to Combine Information or Make It More Useful.* Presenting the network with the price of gold today may help the network forecast the S&P 500 a week from now; however, presenting the network with the *change* in the price of gold over the past week should be much more meaningful to the network.

- *Step 4. Set Minimums and Maximums.* Determine the range of data and set minimum and maximum values to these levels. This makes processing more efficient by focusing the network's attention on the pertinent data—if the data goes from 100 to 200 then the minimums and maximums would be set at 100 and 200 not at −100 and 1000.

- *Step 5. Extract Test Set Data.* In order to be able to test the network with data that it has not seen before, that is, data used for *training* the network, it is common to set aside some of the data set for future testing. Therefore, the total data set is divided into two different sets, one for training and one for testing.

- *Step 6. Select Suitable Network Architecture.* Networks can have three, four, or even five layers; the number of neurons in the hidden layers can vary from one to several hundred. This construction of the network is called the *architecture of the network*. There are more than a dozen known architectures and some are better suited to solving a particular problem than others.

- *Step 7. Select a Suitable Learning (Training) Algorithm.* There are several algorithms (methods of training) that can be used with any particular network architecture. For specific problems, some work better than others.

- *Step 8. Train the Network.* Apply training data to a particular architecture and training algorithm. This adjusts the weights, which connect the neurons, in such a way that the network makes good forecasts when presented with that or similar data sets.

- *Step 9. Use the Network.* Apply new data sets or current data to the trained network to create a forecast.

Despite the exciting capabilities of neural networks, they are not the answer for all problems. As discussed in Chapter 1, if a well-defined mathematical solution exists for a problem, then applying a neural network to that problem is inappropriate.

Neural networks are best applied to problems that require pattern matching, complex interrelationships, or selective use of data. Often the patterns to be discovered by the network are not obvious to a human observer. That the stock market follows the bond market is a well-known financial phenomenon. However, the relationship between gold and the stock market is not as obvious. Neural networks that predict the movement of the stock market are often improved when the price of gold is included as one of the inputs. It adds robustness to the forecast by using the implicit relationship between the price of gold and the movement of the stock market even if we as humans are not able to discern it.

DETERMINING WHAT IS TO BE FORECAST

Determining what is to be forecast is a very crucial and critical part of a successful process. What if we wanted to forecast tomorrow's closing price of the Dow Jones Industrial Average (DJIA). If the DJIA is at approximately 3800 and it changes each day by about 10 points, then this change corresponds to about 0.263 percent. If we intend to forecast the DJIA to an accuracy of plus or minus 2 DJIA points, then we require an accuracy of 0.05 percent (2 points out of 3800). However, if we try to forecast the *change* in DJIA at tomorrow's close instead of the absolute price, then an accuracy of only 20 percent is required (2 points out of 10). That is quite a difference, and it is obtained *simply by viewing the problem differently.*

What if we only need to know whether the market will go *up* or *down* tomorrow and don't really care how far it goes? This is a much easier problem than trying to predict the value of the DJIA at tomorrow's close or even the size of the price change because we have reduced the choice to one of two.

We uncover many different problems when we try to select what to predict. If we want to know the value of the S&P 500 a week from today, do we predict the value one week ahead using weekly data, or do we predict five days in advance using daily data? We might think that daily data would provide more accuracy, but weekly data has less noise when your objective is long term. The answer to this problem can best be determined by building both networks, optimizing the network, training it, and comparing the results of the daily network to the weekly network.

Choosing what to forecast can make a big difference in the results obtained. We will explore this in greater depth in Chapter 3.

SELECTING DATA

Choosing the correct inputs, just as choosing what is to be forecast, can make an important difference in the results. Part of selecting correct inputs is being certain that the data is available in timely fashion. The price of Mongolian bonds might have a large effect on the movement of the stock market, but the data may not be available at the time you need it. Because of the accessibility of historic data, some people forget that non-U.S. statistics are often slow to be released and undependable.

If you want a network to screen mortgage applicants, then the input data may be found in the form of existing mortgage applications. This data can be entered into an electronic spreadsheet, such as Lotus 123™ or Microsoft Excel.™ The spreadsheet columns would represent different categories. The first column might be "salary," the second column might be "years on the job," and the next column might be called "other income." The rows then would represent different mortgage applications.

However, the input data for a stock market forecast is not likely to be found in some file cabinet. Usually, this data is collected through a modem from a data vendor, such as Dow Jones or Dial Data. The data is then imported into a spreadsheet. The columns represent different inputs and the rows represent the time periods.

PREPROCESSING DATA

Spreadsheets can get very large, often reaching 50 columns by 1000 rows (which fills 50,000 cells). When all the data is in the spreadsheet, the data is preprocessed. An example of preprocessing in the spreadsheet for a market forecaster might be to divide the number of advancing issues by the number of declining issues. This quotient now contains the information of the two inputs. Testing has shown that most networks forecast more accurately when presented with the advance/decline quotient rather than the individual inputs.

Another example of preprocessing might be to give the forecast network today's value of DJIA and the values 5 days ago and 10 days ago. Or we might include the 5-day, 20-day, and 50-day moving averages of the DJIA. Frequently we take the original data and manipulate it to extract more information. The data is used to create technical indicators such as the relative strength indicator, or Bollinger Bands. (If you are not familiar with these terms, see the Glossary.)

Another step in preprocessing might be to *normalize* the data. Ten years ago, the Dow Jones Industrial Average was about 1000; today the value is near 4000. One way to treat the wide range is to normalize the data. In most cases, this is accomplished by subtracting a relatively long-term moving average from the data. Figures 2–2 and 2–3 show typical data before and after normalizing. Notice that the normalizing has removed the long-term upward bias in the data and the short-term movements are much more apparent.

Minimum and Maximum Values

When the preprocessing is complete, the spreadsheet is usually imported into the neural network software program or the neural software uses the spreadsheet directly by wrapping itself around the spreadsheet in the form of a shell. It is at this point that the neural

Figure 2–2   Typical time series data. Note the long-term trend. Copyright © 1990 by Ward Systems Group, Inc.

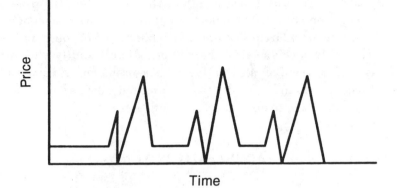

Figure 2–3 Detrended data shows the data after removing long-term trend. This is usually accomplished by subtracting a long-term moving average (say 20 to 50 periods long) from the data. Copyright © 1990 by Ward Systems Group, Inc.

software sets the minimum and maximum values of the inputs by scanning the data. This is necessary in order to scale the inputs to a data range acceptable as input to the network.

Extracting Test Data

Next the data is divided into two or more groups or sets. The first set is the *training* set and the second is the *test* set. Normally about 10 percent of the data is put aside in the test set. The *training* set is data the network uses to find patterns and interrelationships. The *test set* is data reserved to validate the trained network using information the network has not seen during training. Only by testing the trained network with fresh data can the designer or user be sure the network has learned to do the task within the accuracy expected. Sometimes additional data will also be separated into a third set for further testing. Test data can be randomly selected; for example, it can be every 10th pattern or all patterns between two dates. Each method has its advantages, depending on what needs to be proved.

NETWORK ARCHITECTURE

The next step is to choose a suitable network. About 85 percent of all problems are trained on a *back-propagation,* three-layer network. A back-propagation network is one which compares the forecast to the actual and uses the difference to adjust the strength of the interconnections between neurons. One neural network software package has 15 different network architectures available. Some of these architectures are highly specialized in their application. Usually, the initial training will be tried on a three-layer back-propagation network because it has been found to be the easiest and has now become a benchmark for judging the results of other architectures.

TRAINING ALGORITHM

Next it is necessary to choose a *training algorithm:* a formula applied to find relationships and patterns. *Momentum* is the most common algorithm, however, neural network software vendors frequently have their own proprietary algorithm. A majority of the networks are trained on some variation of the momentum algorithm. When these choices have been made, training can begin.

TRAINING AND TESTING

During the training process, input data is presented to the network one row at a time from the spreadsheet. The network then makes a guess as to the correct answer and compares it to the column that contains the correct answer. It records the error, adjusts the strength of the interconnections between the neurons and then goes on to the next row of data and repeats the process. When all data has been scanned, it starts back at the beginning and goes through the data again, and again, and again. Each exposure to the full set of data is called an *epoch.* (See Figure 2–4.) It is not uncommon for the network to look at several thousand epochs, a million rows of data, in the process of comparing results. These rows of data are labeled "facts" by some software companies and "patterns" by others. The process is considered *computer-intensive.*

The interconnections between the neurons are called *weights.* It is the strength of these interconnections that make networks unique. The way two seemingly identical three-layer networks, each with 6 inputs, 6 hidden neurons, and 1 output differ from one another is in the strength of the interconnections between their neurons.

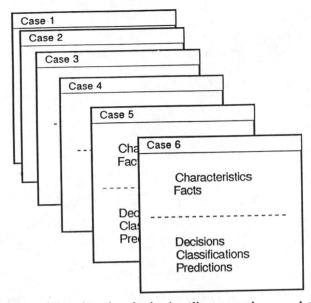

Figure 2–4 Organizing data for the brain. Illustrates the way data might be presented to a human, in an organized way to help learning. Each page represents a fact (pattern). When training a artificial neural network, each row of the spreadsheet represents a fact or pattern. Copyright © 1990 by Ward Systems Group, Inc.

Some software programs test the network periodically during the training process to determine whether the network is sufficiently trained. Periodically (for example, every 200 runs through the data), the training is stopped and the network is checked using the test data. This periodic stopping and testing is continued until the network fails to improve its performance when run on the test data. When further training fails to improve the network, the network configuration is saved and the training is done. If the software package does not have this feature, the network must be periodically manually stopped by the trainer and tested to monitor the training progress.

Figures 2–5 and 2–6 show the error pattern of a network as the training process continues. Notice that the error remains large in the early stages, then improves rapidly until as the end is approached the error reaches a level at which it cannot be reduced. This is where the network stops learning.

If training is continued beyond the point where the learning has stopped, then the network begins to memorize the correct answers,

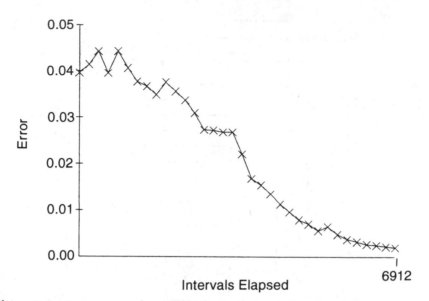

Figure 2–5   Error curve of a network being trained after 6912 learning events. Improvement occurs steadily during the early training period.

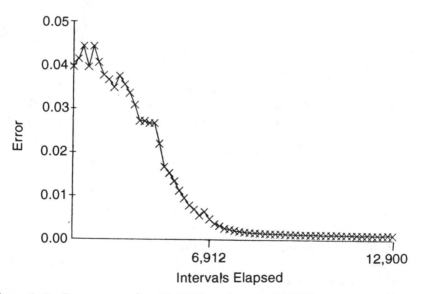

Figure 2–6   Error curve after 12,900 learning events. With twice as many tests as shown in Figure 2–5, there is only little improvement.

and the error begins to increase. Such an overtrained network pre-
forms poorly when tested with new data. It is said that *it does not generalize well.*

REALITY

Frequently, the network does not live up to expectations, that is, it
does not yield the desired accuracy and the designer must rethink
what is to be forecast, the choice of inputs, and the preprocessing.
Many software packages have facilities to see which inputs make a
large contribution to the solution and which inputs add little value to
the solution. This greatly assists the rethinking of the problem.

When the network has been trained to the designer's expectations, the network is ready to be used.

3

Choosing What Is to Be Predicted and Selecting Appropriate Inputs

Although people buy neural network software packages, select an optimistic target to be forecast, provide a broad-brush set of inputs, train a generic network architecture using a generic learning algorithm and have some success, this approach fails to produce the desired profits more often than not.

A much higher success rate comes from the following steps:

1. A studied selection of the target output,

2. Selection of inputs that have predictive relationship to the selected output, and

3. Selection of the optimum neural network architecture and training algorithms.

TIME SERIES FORECASTING—ABSOLUTE VALUE

As discussed in Chapter 2, forecasting the *price* of the DJIA, the OEX or the S&P 500, 5 or 10 periods into the future is usually not a profitable course of action. For example, the Dow, which is currently trading in the 4000 to 4400 range has an average change per week of about

20

20 points, or 0.5 percent. We can find specific weeks where the change was much larger but, on average, the weekly changes fall between 20 to 40 points. To be useful, a network would have to predict the value of the Dow to about 0.1 percent or 4 points. Given the dynamic and volatile behavior of the stock market, this would be an unrealistic goal. It is better to predict some value that is tolerant of a wider margin of error.

For example, if we predict the *change* in the Dow, rather than its price level, the tolerance for error can be much larger. If the average change in the Dow is 20 points and our prediction is within a 20 percent error, we still have our 4-point objective, but the error tolerance has increased dramatically from 0.1 percent to 20 percent. It is a much easier to forecast to 20 percent error tolerance than to a 0.1 percent accuracy.

Some of the variables that can be substituted for the absolute price level in time series prediction include:

1. The recent price change.
2. Whether this most recent data represents a market top or bottom.
3. Whether to buy, sell, or hold.
4. Whether forecast date represents the highest high or lowest low.
5. The change in value over the forecast period.
6. Whether the trend is up or down.
7. The rate of change.
8. The quality of making a trade at this time.
9. Whether the most recent data represents a change in trend.
10. Volatility.
11. Change in volatility.

A BENCHMARK NETWORK

To illustrate the effect of varying various neural network parameters, a *benchmark network* using time-series data will be used. This data consists of 238 hourly readings of the following six items:

1. S&P futures contract (SPY).

2. New York Stock Exchange 100 index (YXY).

3. Number of NYSE advances (ADV).

4. Number of NYSE declines (DEC).

5. Tick volume (TICK).

6. Number of up issues/number of down issues divided by volume of up issues/volume of down issues (TRIN).

This data series is used directly as the inputs to the neural network. Only specified variables (being discussed) will be changed in future applications of this benchmark network.

The benchmark network will use these six inputs—(1) SPY, (2) YXY, (3) ADV, (4) DEC, (5) TICK and (6) TRIN and has the following characteristics:

- The network predicts the SPY five hours in the future.

- The network has 6 neurons in the hidden layer.

- The network has 1 output neuron.

- The network is of the back-propagation type.

- The network is trained using a momentum algorithm with a learn rate of 0.05 and a momentum factor of 0.5.

- After every 200 runs during training, the network is applied to the test data (fresh data previously set aside) and the training stopped when the network can no longer improve its performance on the test data.

Figure 3–1 is the first example of the results of the benchmark network when trained as described. Column A gives the *actual value* of the time series. Column B gives the *network forecast* when trained to the point where no further improvement is possible, and column C gives the *forecast error*. Since this is a very typical network architecture and training algorithm, the results will also serve as a benchmark. We will use this same input data, in a number of different network architectures, learning algorithms and forecast targets, throughout the book. Comparisons will then be made to this benchmark to see whether the changes result in improved network performance.

	A	B	C
1	Actual(1)	Network(1)	Act-Net(1)
2	448.64	449.47	-0.83
3	448.23	449.78	-1.55
4	448.04	450.28	-2.24
5	447.94	449.82	-1.88
6	448.41	449.40	-0.99
7	448.66	449.76	-1.10
8	449.22	449.38	-0.16
9	448.38	449.01	-0.63
10	447.29	448.74	-1.45
11	447.57	448.38	-0.81
12	447.55	448.26	-0.71
13	446.92	448.75	-1.83
14	446.55	448.86	-2.31
15	445.75	449.20	-3.45
16	446.30	447.89	-1.59
17	445.31	447.08	-1.77
18	445.34	447.21	-1.87
19	445.18	447.22	-2.04
20	445.70	446.82	-1.12
21	445.85	446.51	-0.66
22	446.02	445.70	0.32
23	444.22	446.58	-2.36
24	445.79	446.00	-0.21
25	446.75	446.21	0.54
26	447.49	446.13	1.36
27	447.08	446.39	0.69
28	447.08	446.63	0.45
29	447.31	446.76	0.55
30	446.14	445.67	0.47
31	446.48	446.85	-0.37
32	446.26	447.68	-1.42
33	446.46	448.27	-1.81
34	446.23	447.87	-1.64
35	446.39	447.98	-1.59
36	447.18	447.98	-0.80
37	446.44	446.43	0.01
38	447.00	446.80	0.20
39	446.76	446.77	-0.01
40	446.52	447.08	-0.56
41	446.20	446.86	-0.66
42	444.11	446.92	-2.81
43	444.51	447.52	-3.01
44	446.58	446.76	-0.18
45	445.79	447.43	-1.64
46	445.26	446.97	-1.71
47	445.27	446.89	-1.62
48	446.21	446.56	-0.35
49	446.83	445.07	1.76
50	447.10	445.25	1.85
51	448.75	446.61	2.14
52	448.32	445.92	2.40
53	448.42	445.57	2.85
54	448.62	445.65	2.97

Figure 3–1   Test results of benchmark network. Printout of the forecast results of the benchmark system. Column A gives the actual value, column B gives the networks forecast value, and column C gives the difference between the actual value and the forecast value. Column C is also called the network error.

RELATIVE CONTRIBUTION

Figure 3–2 shows the relative contributions of the various inputs to the network. The relative contribution was determined by summing the strength of connections between the input neurons and the neurons in the hidden layer. Inputs that had little effect on the output had weak connections to the hidden layer and conversely, inputs that had a large effect on the output had strong connections to the hidden layer.

In Chapter 4 we will add various inputs and indicators to the benchmark network to determine their efficiency in assisting the network to a more accurate solution.

FORECASTING TIME SERIES DIRECTION—UP OR DOWN

Frequently it is not necessary to know the exact value of a time series at a precise point in the future, but only to know if it is up or down, above or below today's price. To predict whether the cash S&P price (SPY) of the benchmark network would be higher or lower 5 periods from now, a new target forecast was established. This target was zero

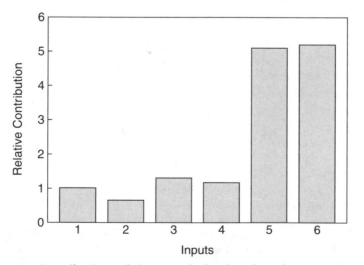

Figure 3–2 Contribution of inputs of the benchmark network. Relative contributions of the 6 inputs to the benchmark network. Input 1 - ADV, input 2 - DEC, input 3 - TICK, input 4 - TRIN, input 5 - SPY, and input 6 - YXY.

if the S&P went down from its value 5 days ago; or plus one (+1) if the target value was up from the value 5 days ago. The same six inputs were used to develop the bench mark network, as shown in Figure 3–3. The target output was 0 or +1 representing up or down expectations, respectively. Training was done in a General Regression Neural Network (GRRN), described in more detail in later chapters. (Note that the back propagation architecture and momentum learning algorithm normally used with the benchmark system does not train well with this particular problem, so the GRNN network was substituted for illustrative purposes only.) The results are shown in Figure 3–3. For interpretation scoring purposes, values between 0.0 and 0.3 were considered as indicating a down movement. Values between 0.31 and 0.69 were considered ambiguous, and values greater than 0.7 forecast an up movement.

Of the 54 sample results shown, 23 were up, 20 were down, and 11 were ambiguous. There was excellent correlation with the input data and 80 percent of the time the network gave the correct prediction.

PERCENT CHANGE IN TIME SERIES DIRECTION

Another approach to forecasting is to predict the percent change over the forward time period. In Figure 3–4, we used the benchmark's six inputs, architecture and learning algorithm to forecast the percentage change for 5-periods ahead.

The values in column A are the actual percentage change over the 5-day period. Column B shows the networks forecast, and column C the difference between the actual percentage change and the forecast percentage change, or the error. In column D, the forecast percentage change has been converted to S&P points for comparison with the benchmark network's forecast of value 5 days in the future (as in Figure 3–1). Column E of Figure 3–4 shows the forecast error converted from percent to S&P points.

The benchmark network had an error range from +2.97 to −3.45. This is a total range of 6.42 points. In the network that forecast the percentage change (Figure 3–3), the range of errors varies from +2.48 to −1.89, a range of 4.37 points, and a 32 percent improvement over the absolute value forecast. We can conclude that predicting the percent change rather than absolute price results in a significant improvement in forecasting accuracy in this particular case.

	A	B
1	Actual(1)	Network(1)
2	1.00	1.00
3	1.00	0.99
4	1.00	1.00
5	1.00	0.99
6	1.00	1.00
7	1.00	0.99
8	1.00	0.99
9	1.00	0.49
10	1.00	0.47
11	1.00	0.34
12	1.00	0.32
13	1.00	0.39
14	1.00	0.43
15	1.00	0.51
16	1.00	0.91
17	1.00	0.98
18	1.00	0.90
19	1.00	0.91
20	1.00	0.97
21	1.00	0.63
22	0.00	0.00
23	1.00	0.72
24	0.00	0.06
25	0.00	0.13
26	0.00	0.17
27	0.00	0.14
28	0.00	0.25
29	0.00	0.32
30	0.00	0.0000
31	0.00	0.51
32	1.00	0.96
33	1.00	0.91
34	1.00	0.87
35	1.00	0.89
36	1.00	0.92
37	0.00	0.05
38	0.00	0.19
39	0.00	0.15
40	0.00	0.28
41	1.00	0.26
42	1.00	0.32
43	1.00	0.58
44	0.00	0.19
45	1.00	0.63
46	1.00	0.42
47	1.00	0.39
48	0.00	0.25
49	0.00	0.000000
50	0.00	0.000
51	0.00	0.12
52	0.00	0.00
53	0.00	0.01
54	0.00	0.12

Figure 3–3   Up/down forecasts. Column B shows results of training the benchmark network to predict whether the SPY would be up or down 5 periods from now. Column A is the actual result where 1 is up and 0 is down.

	A	B	C	D	E
1	Actual(1)	Network(1)	Act-Net(1)	VALUE	ERROR
2	0.00	0.47	-0.47		
3	0.00	0.38	-0.38		
4	0.00	0.36	-0.36		
5	0.00	0.27	-0.27		
6	0.00	0.20	-0.20		
7	0.06	0.22	-0.16	0.99	-0.72
8	-0.04	0.19	-0.23	0.86	-1.04
9	-0.52	-0.14	-0.39	-0.63	-1.76
10	-0.55	-0.13	-0.42	-0.59	-1.89
11	-0.58	-0.16	-0.42	-0.72	-1.89
12	-0.57	-0.17	-0.40	-0.77	-1.80
13	-0.37	-0.12	-0.25	-0.54	-1.13
14	0.00	-0.07	0.07	-0.32	0.32
15	0.22	-0.02	0.25	-0.09	1.13
16	0.08	-0.14	0.21	-0.63	0.95
17	-0.15	-0.26	0.11	-1.17	0.50
18	-0.19	-0.24	0.05	-1.08	0.23
19	-0.25	-0.24	-0.00	-1.08	0.00
20	-0.51	-0.29	-0.23	-1.31	-1.04
21	-0.41	-0.24	-0.17	-1.08	-0.77
22	-0.34	-0.22	-0.12	-0.99	-0.54
23	-0.28	-0.12	-0.17	-0.54	-0.77
24	-0.50	-0.22	-0.28	-0.99	-1.26
25	-0.35	-0.15	-0.21	-0.67	-0.95
26	-0.31	-0.17	-0.14	-0.77	-0.63
27	-0.01	-0.12	0.11	-0.54	0.50
28	-0.10	-0.11	0.01	-0.50	0.05
29	0.16	-0.07	0.23	-0.32	1.04
30	-0.25	-0.22	-0.03	-0.99	-0.14
31	0.14	-0.04	0.18	-0.18	0.81
32	0.24	0.08	0.16	0.36	0.72

Figure 3–4 Percentage change forecast. Results of training network to forecast the percentage change expected rather than a value or change in value. Refer to the text for detailed explanation as to what each column represents.

The choice of the proper variable to predict can make a big difference in the results. Often it is necessary to try several different outputs to see which yields the best forecast. Frequently, suitable input data is not available in a timely and easily procured manner. When this occurs, it is sometimes necessary to modify the forecast target to fit the available data. While selecting the right target to be forecast is very important, it is also highly dependent on the availability of inputs that have a predictive relationship to the chosen target output.

TIME HORIZON

The time horizon of the forecast, that is, whether it is long term or short term, enters into to the selection of the item to be forecast. Table 3–1 shows the results of a GRNN network and a back-propagation network over increasing forecast periods from 1 to 100 days. Results are expressed as R-squared, higher values indicating greater accuracy. The input data was the data of the benchmark network described earlier. The vertical axis in Figure 3–5 is the R-squared value of the network,

Table 3–1   Comparison of two architectures when period is varied. Resulting values of R-squared are shown, the correlation between actual and forecast values, when forecast period is varied for two different network architectures.

Forecast Periods	Type of Network	
	GRNN	Backpro
1	0.9740	0.981
2	0.9695	0.965
3	0.9495	0.923
4	0.9564	0.912
5	0.9509	0.909
6	0.9766	0.900
8	0.9893	(0.887)
10	0.985	0.873
15	0.976	0.855
20	0.959	0.852
35	0.952	0.869
50	0.910	0.788
100	0.804	0.684

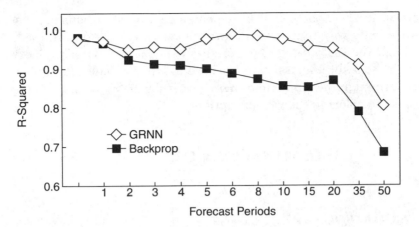

Figure 3–5 R-squared values for two different network architectures when forecasting for different periods. The backpropagation decays through period 6. Longer periods are difficult to forecast.

and the horizontal axis gives the number of periods ahead in the forecast. To show how the importance of selecting the correct or best variables, the two different network solutions are shown together in the Figure 3–5. The benchmark system that used back-propagation is plotted as squares. As expected, the R-square value falls as the forecast period lengthens, showing that it is more difficult to produce a longer term forecast.

The line shown with diamonds is the R-squared values using the benchmark network inputs with a General Regression Neural Network (GRNN) (network architectures are discussed in greater detail in Chapter 5). After the second period, this network yields much better R-squared values than the benchmark network. Note that after dropping off slightly for the 2-, 3-, 4-period ranges, the R-squared values climb and reach a peak in the 8-period range, then slowly fall to the 15-period forecast. In fact, the 15-period results of the GRNN network are better than the results obtained using the benchmark system during the 1 through 5 periods.

Not only is the profitability of a given neural network affected by the selection of the forecast target, but also by the forecasted period and the selection of network architecture. Only by testing for the correlations of various periods can the optimum forecast time period be determined. As we discuss further in Chapter 5, the selection of the architecture and learning algorithm can have a large effect on the accuracy of the network. Repeated testing of various approaches is the only way that the *optimum* network can be determined. Although the thrown-together, fresh-out-of-the-box, first-try network might be a success, a network where all the variables have been optimized might be many times more profitable, more than repaying the costs of exploring the various options.

OTHER NEURAL NETWORK APPLICATIONS

Stock Selection

A highly profitable application of neural networks to financial forecasting is picking which security is most likely to go up in value. One approach to picking stocks out of a large universe would be to forecast a relative ranking. Poor choices might get a rating of 0 to 3, good choices might be rated 7 to 10.

Mortgage Applicants

Another useful neural network forecast is the grading of mortgage applicants. The targets would range from 0, for past applicants who were bad risks to +1 for applicants who were good risks. This problem is very similar to the problem for forecasting whether the stock market would go up or down.

Bankruptcy Forecasts

Bank failure and bankruptcy predictions are very similar to the stock market up/down and the mortgage application problems and are probably best served by a 0/+1, or Fail/Pass forecast target.

Bond Grading

The grading of bonds, although similar to forecasting bank or business failure, is complicated by the fact that acceptable bonds can have any of five ratings. Standard and Poors uses the rating scheme shown in Table 3–2. Moody, which also rates bonds, uses a similar rating

Table 3-2 Possible bond rating system.

	Equal Rating	Favors Junk
AAA	4.00	7.00 and up
AA	3.00–3.99	6.00–6.99
A	2.00–2.99	5.00–5.99
BBB	1.00–1.99	4.00–4.99
CCC	0.00–0.99	0.00–3.99

scheme with different letter designations. We will use the following notation.

AAA	Highest Rating
AA	Very close to AAA rating
A	Good, susceptible to adverse conditions
BBB	Adequate, more susceptible to conditions
CCC	"JUNK" bonds

A possible forecast target for rating bonds might be one of the ones shown in Table 3-2.

The column of possible output parameters titled Equal Rating gives approximately equal rating to each bond category and the column labeled favors junk gives more emphasis to the junk bonds. It is very possible that neither of these schemes is the best. Instead one that gave more emphasis to the grades AA to BBB might yield greater accuracy. It is only by trying the different assignment methods that the best one can be located.

In training such networks, it will be important that each bond-rating category have an equally large number of training patterns. That is, the number of training patterns in the AAA category should equal the number of training patterns in the AA category, and so forth. If mostly AAA, AA, and A training patterns are presented and only a few BBB and CCC patterns, then the network will know little about BBB and CCC patterns except by inference, rather then by first-hand experience.

4

INPUT SELECTION

This chapter covers selecting appropriate inputs and methods of testing the selected inputs to be sure that they have a predictive relationship to what is being forecast. In addition, suitable inputs for various common forecasting problems are presented.

SELECTING APPROPRIATE INPUTS

The selection of inputs having a predictive relationship to the target is as important as the selection of the best possible target to be forecast. Selecting inputs to determine which mortgage applicants are most likely to default is a relatively easy task. Choosing the inputs for forecasting the S&P five days in the future is a much more difficult job. Forecasting the S&P 500 five days in advance is more difficult because both the inputs and the target outputs used for time-series forecasting are very noisy. That is, the data has a lot of excessive, or "random" movement that has nothing to do with overall direction or trend.

The data used for rating mortgage applicants tends to be more generalized. If there is no income to make the monthly payments, the applicant will default on the loan, and it is relatively easy for the network to recognize this. In time-series forecasting, an input value can gap up today, and promptly come back down tomorrow and remain down for the next month. Was the jump today an important piece of information or just noise? Because the input stayed down for the next month, we can surmise that it was noise, or a random movement, only *after* the fact.

CORRELATION AND CONTRIBUTION

Many neural network software programs incorporate one or more subprograms to assist in the selection of suitable inputs. These subprograms allow a given input to be compared to the target to determine whether a predictive relationship exists. That is, it determines the *correlation* of the designated input to the variable to be forecast. This subprogram frequently gives a scatter plot of the relationship of the two variables being tested, so the relationship can be easily seen and assessed. Figure 4–1 shows the Gold and Silver Mining Index plotted against the volume on the New York Stock Exchange. As you can see, there is no correlation at all, because the scatter diagram has no form. A classic lack of correlation appears as a circle when plotted. Figure 4–2 shows the Dow Transportation Index plotted against the OEX (S&P 100). Here we have very good correlation as shown by the elongated pattern that moves diagonally towards the upper right corner.

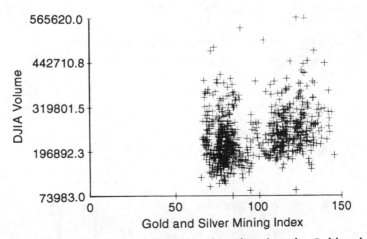

Figure 4–1 Scatter graph of DJIA volume plotted against the Gold and Silver Mining Index. The lack of form indicates that there is no relationship between the items being compared.

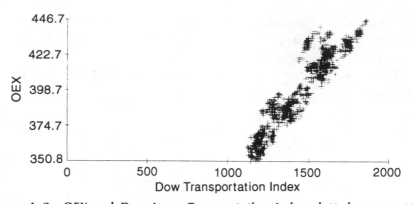

Figure 4–2 OEX and Dow Jones Transportation Index plotted as a scatter graph. The elongated form shows that there is a relationship between these two variables. A straight line would indicate a perfect relationship. The width of the band is a measure of noice and real differences between the two indices.

A second tool sometimes included in neural network software programs is a subprogram that determines the *contribution* of each input to the target *after* the network is trained. This is usually accomplished by adding all the weights connected to each input. Inputs with a large total of weights are more significant than an input with only a small total of weights.

Table 4–1 shows the results obtained by running both a correlation and a contribution subprogram on the benchmark case described in Chapter 3. *The actual value of the SPY 5 periods in advance was forecast.*

With correlation factors below 10 percent, the ADV, DEC, TRIN, and TICK would normally not qualify as inputs to the network.

Table 4–1 Shows the correlation of the inputs to the output of the benchmark network. The third column shows the contribution to the the solution of the various inputs. See text for fuller explanation.

	Input	Correlation	Contribution
(#1)	ADV	8.2%	1.7 or 13%
(#2)	DEC	3.2%	1.5 or 12%
(#3)	TRIN	8.9%	1.4 or 11%
(#4)	TICK	5.6%	1.6 or 13%
(#5)	SPY	96.0%	3.2 or 25%
(#6)	YXY	96.0%	3.3 or 26%

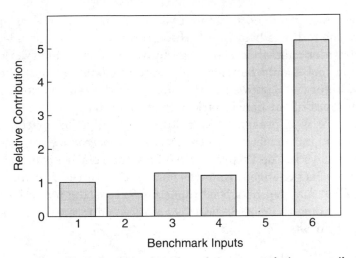

Figure 4–3 Contribution of the benchmark inputs. Relative contribution of benchmark inputs when forecasting value of SPY 5 periods in the future. The number of the inputs corresponds to the numbers in Table 4–1.

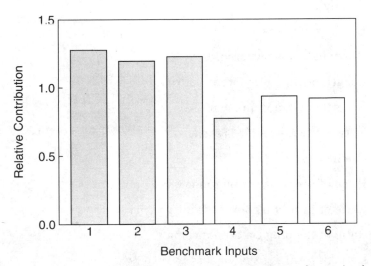

Figure 4–4 Benchmark inputs forecasting the percentage change in the SPY. Relative contribution of benchmark inputs when forecasting the percentage change of the SPY 5 periods in advance. Compare to Figure 4–3.

However, when judged by their total contribution level of approximately one half the best input, these inputs must be included. This demonstrates that when choosing inputs for a neural network, every selection tool should be used and every reasonable input should be tested. Figure 4–3 shows in graphical form the relative contribution of each input of the benchmark network as a bar.

Figure 4–4 presents the relative contribution of these same benchmark inputs when used to forecast the *percentage change* of the SPY five days in the future. Notice how the relative contribution of each input has changed from its contribution in the benchmark network. What may not be a good input for forecasting a particular target can become the most important input when forecasting a slightly different target.

MORTGAGE UNDERWRITING

Although the mortgage application problem seems relatively simple, particularly with regard to selection of the inputs, defining "good" and "bad" loans requires difficult value judgments. Some possible inputs for a mortgage underwriting network might be:

- Family income.
- Family expenses.
- Previous home ownership.
- Length of time at current address.
- Length of time in present job.
- Future prospects for present job.
- Credit report.
- Ratio of property value to mortgage amount.
- Ratio of family income to family expenses.
- Ratio of housing costs to income.
- Ratio of total debt payments to income.
- Portion of income from sources other than salary.

- Probability that other income would continue.

- Source of downpayment: savings? parental gift?

- Downpayment as percent of purchase price.

- Past history of bankruptcy.

- Number of dependents.

- Employment status (self-employed, salaried).

- Who will occupy the property.

- Loan amount.

- Age of property.

- Number of units.

- Appraised value.

- Property location.

Because mortgages are long-term obligations during which time much can go wrong, defining a good or bad loan application is a difficult problem. If the loan is bad, it may be years before it goes into default. Some possible approaches to selecting a target output are:

1. Use the judgment of one or more very senior and experienced loan officers to define probable good and bad mortgage applications.

2. Loans usually do not go bad in the first three months; three to five years is more likely. Therefore, use applications from five or even ten years ago. What criteria do we use to define a bad loan? For example, it may be significant if the applicant was late on one payment, or if a prior loan goes to foreclosure. Again, the advice of experienced loan officers should be relied on to determine the criteria that should be used to flag a bad loan.

3. If we use applications from five years ago to train the network, we need to consider how economic conditions have changed over the intervening period. Are the terms, interest rates, and downpayment requirements comparable to current loans? Is the outlook for economic conditions the same as five years ago?

In order for the mortgage network to train properly, it should be exposed to equal amounts of data on acceptable applications (those which a senior and experienced loan officer would accept) and unacceptable applications (those which the same loan officer would decline). In addition to training on conventional three-layer back-propagation networks, it might pay to experiment by training the data on different network architectures such as Kohonen, Probabilistic Neural Networks (PNN), and General Regression Neural Networks (GRNN) to see if better R-squares, that is, more accurate forecasts, can be obtained. Chapter 7 will cover network architectures in more detail.

BANK FAILURES

The items that follow make excellent inputs to networks that forecast bank and thrift failures. These inputs perform best when used as ratios to assets, total loans and total deposits where appropriate. Ratios perform better than raw inputs because they generalize the values.

Capital	Interest paid
Agricultural loans	Net income
Commercial loans	Total assets
Individual loans	Total expenses
Real estate loans	Cash or cash equivalents
Loans past due	Net worth
Provision for bad loans	Repossessed assets

The forecast output should use the range 0 to +1, where 0 indicates failed bank and +1 indicates a bank or thrift in the best of health that is not expected to fail in the near to intermediate future. As always when training the bank failure network, different network architectures should be tried.

As with the network for judging mortgage applications, it is important that an equal number good banks and failed banks are present in the data, so the network gets exposure to an equal number of strong and weak banks. It is the tendency of network designers to present an overwhelming proportion of strong banks and a few weak banks to the network, because that is the normal distribution of the data. There is also the phenomenon of "selection bias" which makes information on previously failed banks less available.

BUSINESS FAILURE

Business failure is a problem very similar to the bank failure problem described in the previous example. The same output and network architecture remarks apply. Typical inputs would be presented as ratios to total assets, total sales, and/or total liabilities. A partial list might include:

Total assets	Inventory
Working capital	Fixed assets
Earnings	Short-term liabilities
Sales	Long-term liabilities
Retained earnings	Short-term assets
Cash and cash equivalents	Long-term assets

BOND RATING

Bond rating, although similar to forecasting bank or business failures, is complicated by the fact that at least four different rating categories are required. Inputs similar to those given for business failure will be applicable to this problem. Some practitioners may want to develop several networks, one to grade the bonds into the four categories, AA, A , B, C, and other networks to grade the bonds within each category.

REAL ESTATE APPRAISAL/PROPERTY TAX ANALYSIS

The target output for real estate is selling price. To show how intricate this problem can be, some of the suitable inputs are:

Lot size—square feet	Appliances
Living space—square feet	Stove
Living space—volume cubic feet	Microwave
Number of bathrooms	Refrigerator
Number of half baths	Dishwasher
Number of bedrooms	Washing machine
Eat-in kitchen	Clothes dryer

Breakfast nook
Dining room
Living room
Family room
Center hall
Patio
Deck
Single house
Duplex
Garden apartment
High-rise apartment
Townhouse
Basement
Finished basement
  Does basement leak
  Sump pump
Condition of roof
Central air conditioning
  Ground sump heat pump
  Water with cooling tower
  Air cooled
Room air conditioning
  Number of rooms
  All living space
Type of heat
  Forced hot air
  Baseboard
  Radiators
Thermopane windows
Garage—How many cars
Landscaping
  Barely
  Passable
  Nice
  Done by architect
Neighborhood, scale 1 to 10
Comparable sales in dollars
Appearance, scale 1 to 10

Special features
  Wrap-around driveway
  Pond
  Stream
  Isolated from neighbors
  Outside lighting
  Security
  Decorative features
  Swimming pool
  Tile entry floor
  Coat closet
  Walk-in closets
  Cedar closet
  Separate laundry
  Basement sink
  Outside faucet
  Paved driveway
  Radiant heating
Humidifier
Dehumidifier
Type of furnace
  Gas
  Oil
  Coal
  Wood stove
  Propane
  Number of zones
Cost to heat
Cost to cool
Sidewalks
Storm sewers
Sanitary sewers
Curbs
Burglar alarm
Zoning
Fireplace
Fire alarm
Smoke detectors

It is necessary to periodically add new data and retrain the network to take care of the effects of inflation.

TIME-SERIES FORECASTING

Inputs for time-series forecasting, which in our case means forecasting stock or index prices into the future, can be separated into two groups. The first are inputs based on fundamental factors. These include the price of gold, $/yen, $/British pound, $/German mark, oil, 3-month Treasury bill, 30-year bond, gross national product (GNP), inflation, government policy, and other similar indicators and values.

The second group contains *technical indicators,* and includes items such as volatility, relative strength index (RSI), average directional movement (ADX), daily high, low, and closing prices, momentum, money flow index, moving averages, on-balance volume, stochastic oscillator, Bollinger Bands, and similar indicators derived from the price and/or volume action of the item to be forecast.

Building a successful neural network using just technical indicators is a difficult task (an example can be found in the Appendix, Case Study 1). Building a successful neural network using fundamental data, if all the parameters are tested and maximized, has a greater chance of success. Adding technical indicators to a fundamental network can, on occasion, result in a network improvement.

To show the affect of various technical indicators, we are going to add them one at a time as a seventh input to our benchmark network and then look at the contribution graph to see its effect. Because we have increased the inputs from 6 to 7, we are also going to increase the neurons in the hidden network from 6 to 7. For reference, the six input benchmark network had an R-squared of 0.9262.

Figures 4–4 through to 4–14 show the contributions of the original six inputs plus the seventh technical input.

Compare these graphs to Figure 4–4 which is a graph of the 6 inputs as used in the benchmark system. Comparing Figure 4–6 to 4–4 shows a remarkable difference. It is readily apparent that the contribution of a given input is dependent on the other inputs that are present. Also note that three of the networks had worse R-square values than the benchmark system. This shows that the addition of some inputs actually degrades the network. It has been a neural network

Table 4–2 Variation of R^2 (error) with different inputs. Each input was added as a seventh input to the benchmark network.

Test #	7th Input	R-Squared
1	5-Period lag of SPY	0.9327
2	10-Period moving average less 5-period moving average	0.9302
3	Momentum	0.9302
4	% Width of Bollinger band	0.9284
5	Stochastic	0.9283
6	10-Period moving average	0.9292
7	Moving average convergence/divergence	0.9278
8	10-Period lag of SPY	0.9278
9	5-Period moving average	0.9240
10	12-Period moving average of RSI	0.9169
11	12-Period relative strength index (RSI)	0.9167

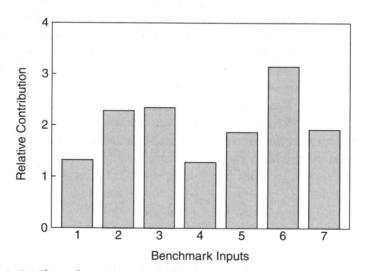

Figure 4–5 First of a series of graphs showing the effect of adding various technical indicators to the benchmark network. In each case, the 7th column is the added indicator. The other 6 inputs are those of the benchmark network. R-squared values are given for each network. For reference, the benchmark network had an R-squared of 0.9262. For this graph, a 5-period lag of the SPY was added as the seventh input. The R-squared value is 0.9327.

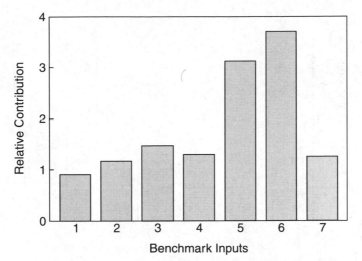

Figure 4–6 Here a 5-period moving average of SPY was subtracted from a 10-period moving average of SPY and the difference was used as the seventh input. The R-squared value was 0.9302.

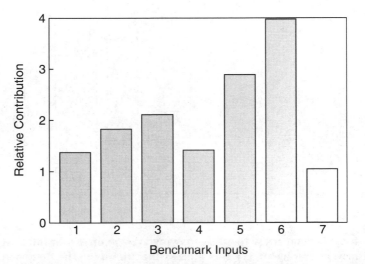

Figure 4–7 Benchmark with a momentum indicator. For this graph, a 12-period momentum indicator of the SPY was added as the 7th input. The R-squared value was 0.9302. Notice that the relative contribution of inputs 2 and 3 varies greatly between Figures 4–5, 4–6, and 4–7.

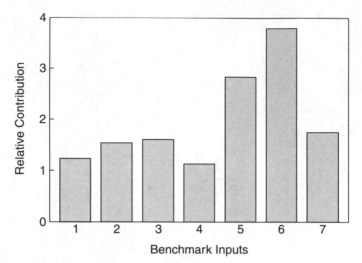

Figure 4–8 Benchmark with 14-period stochastic. Here a 14-period stochastic indicator smoothed with a 3-period moving average is used as the 7th input. The R-squared value is 0.9283.

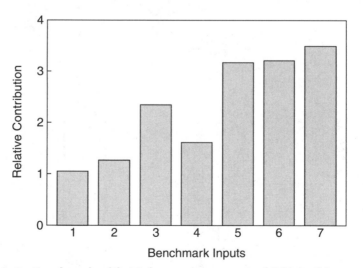

Figure 4–9 Benchmark with 10 day moving average of SPY. In this case, a 10-period moving average of SPY was used as the 7th input. The R-squared value was 0.9292. Compare the relative contributions of the 7th inputs in this and the previous figures. They could not be more different. Yet the R-squared values differ by only one number in the third place. Also notice the difference between inputs 3 and 5.

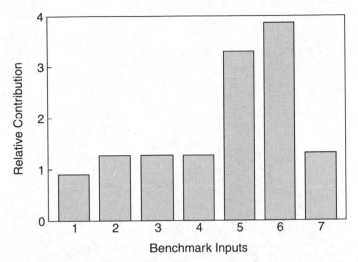

Figure 4–10 Benchmark with the MACD as a 7th input. Here a Moving Average Convergence/Divergence Indicator (MACD) is used as the 7th input. Notice the difference in the relative contributions to the previous graph, Figure 4–9. The R-squared value is 0.9278.

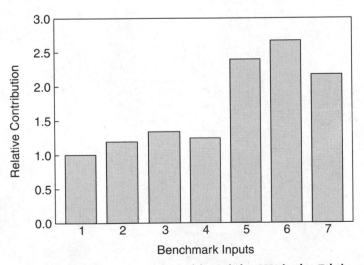

Figure 4–11 Benchmark with 10-period lag of the SPY is the 7th input. The R-squared value is 0.9278.

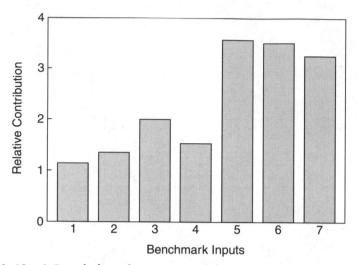

Figure 4–12 A 5-period moving average of the SPY as the 7th input. The R-squared value is 0.9240.

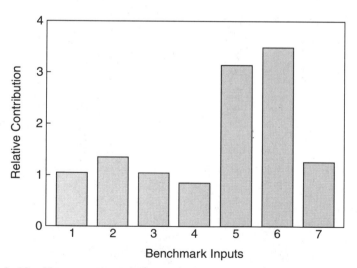

Figure 4–13 Here a 12-period moving average of a 12-period Relative Strength Index (RSI) is the 7th input. The R-squared value is a lowly 0.9169.

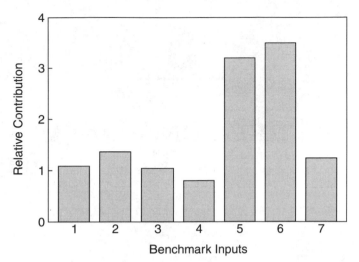

Figure 4–14 Benchmark with 12-period RSI. A 12-period Relative Strength Index (RSI) is the 7th input and the R-squared value is 0.9167. Compare the relative contribution of this graph with some of the earlier graph. Notice how the relative contribution of the various inputs varies with the choice of the 7th input. This shows that the value of any particular input can depend greatly on the choice of the other inputs.

axiom that it was acceptable to add inputs because the net work itself would learn to ignore those that did not contribute anything. It is probable that the inputs that degraded the network were colinear with one of the other inputs.

Once again we see that developing the optimum network requires great care in selecting the inputs and then testing those chosen to be sure the optimum mix has been selected. Logical, intelligent selection of the inputs is a key ingredient to a robust solution.

5

PREPARING DATA

This chapter bridges the gap between selecting the inputs and training the network. It shows how the inputs are imported into a spreadsheet. It also shows how data is manipulated in various ways to improve the ultimate performance of the network.

SPREADSHEETS

Input and output data is presented to the network in spreadsheet form. The columns represent the input categories such as the price of gold, silver, S&P 500, or corn. The rows represent other data of corresponding time periods, that is, the price value each quarter, month, day, or hour.

Figure 5–1 shows rows 1-50 of a spreadsheet for the benchmark network. Notice that the column labeled *Lag(5) of SPY* has no data for rows 2 through 6. This is because lags are created by shifting the data down the appropriate number of rows needed to perform a calculation or reference prior data. This particular neural network software program uses an asterisk to tell the network to ignore these rows because the data is incomplete. In some neural network programs, these incomplete rows must be deleted. Moving averages also

	A	B	C	D	E	F	G	H
1	ADV	DEC	TICK	TRIN	SPY	YXY	Lead(5) of SPY	Lag(5) of SPY
2	994.00	540.00	426.00	0.86	450.23	249.42	450.50	
3	1070.00	625.00	88.00	0.79	450.28	249.41	450.08	
4	1144.00	663.00	248.00	0.81	451.00	249.71	448.64	
5	1122.00	687.00	153.00	0.95	450.70	249.58	448.23	
6	1201.00	703.00	252.00	1.06	450.65	249.57	448.04	
7	1213.00	740.00	112.00	0.88	450.50	249.49	447.94	450.23
8	1214.00	781.00	31.00	0.91	450.08	249.26	448.41	450.28
9	668.00	809.00	-39.00	0.91	448.64	248.69	448.66	451.00
10	729.00	924.00	-12.00	0.91	448.23	248.50	449.22	450.70
11	777.00	965.00	12.00	1.01	448.04	248.44	448.38	450.65
12	790.00	1012.00	-2.00	1.02	447.94	248.31	447.29	450.50
13	838.00	1048.00	28.00	0.98	448.41	248.52	447.57	450.08
14	892.00	1008.00	85.00	0.98	448.66	248.70	447.55	448.64
15	938.00	1002.00	109.00	0.97	449.22	248.83	446.92	448.23
16	688.00	764.00	-74.00	1.31	448.38	248.62	446.55	448.04
17	718.00	919.00	-125.00	1.52	447.29	248.10	445.75	447.94
18	774.00	961.00	38.00	1.45	447.57	248.20	446.30	448.41
19	807.00	976.00	-36.00	1.52	447.55	248.21	445.31	448.66
20	804.00	1043.00	-94.00	1.60	446.92	247.90	445.34	449.22
21	812.00	1071.00	84.00	1.71	446.55	247.76	445.18	448.38
22	904.00	1005.00	115.00	1.80	445.75	247.42	445.70	447.29
23	724.00	763.00	40.00	1.00	446.30	247.59	445.85	447.57
24	724.00	926.00	-110.00	1.08	445.31	247.15	446.02	447.55
25	760.00	989.00	-32.00	0.96	445.34	247.11	444.22	446.92
26	786.00	1038.00	-153.00	0.97	445.18	246.99	445.79	446.55
27	809.00	1046.00	61.00	0.98	445.70	247.20	446.75	445.75
28	834.00	1070.00	-63.00	0.93	445.85	247.23	447.49	446.30
29	855.00	1060.00	-10.00	0.90	446.02	247.32	447.08	445.31
30	544.00	985.00	-235.00	0.90	444.22	246.41	447.08	445.34
31	675.00	1031.00	0.00	0.78	445.79	247.04	447.31	445.18
32	722.00	1010.00	104.00	0.69	446.75	247.47	446.14	445.70
33	777.00	1025.00	28.00	0.70	447.49	247.78	446.48	445.85
34	821.00	1049.00	7.00	0.71	447.08	247.58	446.26	446.02
35	830.00	1075.00	-54.00	0.68	447.08	247.57	446.46	444.22
36	871.00	1056.00	88.00	0.71	447.31	247.69	446.23	445.79
37	648.00	831.00	-119.00	1.03	446.14	247.20	446.39	446.75
38	729.00	923.00	-31.00	0.97	446.48	247.34	447.18	447.49
39	740.00	995.00	-80.00	0.96	446.26	247.24	446.44	447.08
40	787.00	1044.00	-91.00	0.88	446.46	247.29	447.00	447.08
41	802.00	1085.00	-182.00	0.93	446.23	247.16	446.76	447.31
42	842.00	1078.00	-103.00	0.91	446.39	247.22	446.52	446.14
43	903.00	1054.00	40.00	0.86	447.18	247.61	446.20	446.48
44	672.00	808.00	-45.00	0.90	446.44	247.27	444.11	446.26
45	750.00	878.00	8.00	0.79	447.00	247.53	444.51	446.46
46	813.00	918.00	-114.00	0.92	446.76	247.37	446.58	446.23
47	811.00	974.00	-171.00	0.92	446.52	247.26	445.79	446.39
48	820.00	1035.00	-165.00	0.99	446.20	247.08	445.26	447.18
49	757.00	1199.00	-535.00	1.19	444.11	246.12	445.27	446.44
50	770.00	1207.00	-265.00	1.17	444.51	246.17	446.21	447.00

Figure 5–1   Small section of typical neural network spreadsheet.

result in incomplete rows. If a 10-day moving average is created, then the first 9 rows of data are incomplete, and appropriate steps need to be taken so that this data is not used by the network.

The item to be forecast is created in a similar manner, only in this case the data is moved up 5 rows because we are forecasting 5 days ahead. This leaves 5 rows at the bottom of the spreadsheet that are incomplete. Steps must be taken so that this data is not used by the network.

CONSTRUCTION OF THE SPREADSHEET

To construct the spreadsheet, we must first collect data. This is usually done by dialing a data vendor such as Dow Jones or Dial Data using a modem and downloading the required historic data (for example, the price of gold from March 1, 1990 to the present). This data is stored in a file. If the price of silver is also required, that information is downloaded and stored in a separate file. If the price of corn is an input, this data too is downloaded to yet another file. Sometimes, the data needed cannot be obtained from a data vendor and must be entered into the spreadsheet manually. This is a procedure that can prove very tiresome although it can represent valuable proprietary data.

Data is frequently obtained by exporting it from a technical analysis program such as Metastock; exporting it saves the data collection process. Exported data may be in the form of a text file rather than a data file. In a text file, data is not divided into separate columns. A text file can be made into a useful data file by means of the spreadsheet's *parsing* function, which breaks the data into separate columns. The parsing function is surprisingly good and can distinguish between data, dates, and text information. However, dates will not be in the month, day, year sequence that is normal, but rather will be presented as the sequential day of the century, that is, how many days since January 1, 1900.

After all the input data has been collected in separate files, the *file combine function* of the spreadsheet is used to place the various inputs in side-by-side columns within the spreadsheet.

It is *very important* that each date be preserved along with the data. When all the files have been combined into one large spreadsheet, the data is examined line-by-line to be sure that all the dates and times are aligned. Markets have unique reporting schedules, therefore there will not be matching data for every time period. For example, the Japanese stock markets have different holidays than the U.S. stock, bond, and commodities markets; these gaps must be resolved. The normal way to deal with missing data is to repeat the data from before omission; another popular method averages the data across the gap. Some neural network architectures require that the data be presented in time sequence with no missing rows, therefore estimating one data item is a much better solution than deleting a full row of data, which results in an artificial gap, and lost information.

PREPROCESSING DATA

Once the data has been imported, parsed, and checked for date correctness, it is preprocessed. This may be done using a conventional spreadsheet, or the data can be imported into the spreadsheet of the neural network software and then preprocessed. Some neural network software packages are shells that wrap around conventional spreadsheets. Other programs incorporate spreadsheets or have the ability to import the data from conventional spreadsheets. If a particular neural network software package does not have a technical analysis package, and it is not possible to import indicators from a technical analysis software package, the technical analysis formulas must then be entered directly into the spreadsheet.

In Chapter 3, it was shown that networks were improved when the *change in value of the inputs* are used rather than the *absolute value*. Similarly, forecasts are much better when the *change in input value* is used as an input rather than the *absolute value*. This type of modification of the inputs is called *preprocessing*. Preprocessing has much to do with how well a network performs. Proper preprocessing can make the difference between a good network and a bad network.

Preprocessing has several advantages:

1. *It extracts the information that has real value to the network.* For example, presenting the change in value instead of the absolute value improves the forecasting ability. The network is able to use change to produce a better forecast. When the absolute value is used, only a small percentage of the value has meaning to the network.

2. *Two variables can be reduced into one input which has more value to the network than the two original variables.* For example, the quotient resulting from dividing the number of advancing issues by the number of declining issues may have more value to the network than using the advancing and declining issues as separate inputs. This process frequently generalizes the data. In addition, two variables have been reduced to one. Since the number

of inputs to a network tend to expand rather than contract, any opportunity to combine two inputs should be taken. This will reduce processing time.

Among the possible ways to preprocess the data are telescoping, subtracting, dividing, moving averages, multiplication, and addition. There are also numerous technical studies that can be included as inputs. See Appendix C for a list of technical analysis studies supplied with one software program that can be used to preprocess the data.

Telescoping Inputs—Lags

Telescoping inputs describes the practice of presenting data from previous time periods. For example, if we are forecasting the price of gold 5 days in advance, we might use the following telescoped inputs:

Gold's value today
5 days ago
10 days ago
15 days ago
20 days ago

Figure 5–2 shows the effect of adding a 5-period lag of each of the 6 inputs to the benchmark network. That is to say, the data consists of the original 6 inputs, plus the value of the input 5 periods ago. Notice that inputs 7 to 12, the lagged inputs contribute almost as much information to the network as the original 6 inputs.

Moving Averages

Moving averages are a useful preprocessing technique. Short-term, 2- to 5-period moving averages, are often substituted for the raw data because they smooth out noise, the random component of the data. At the other extreme, longer term moving averages can simulate a fundamental trend. Figure 5–3 shows the contribution of 4-, 9-, and 18-period moving averages when added to the benchmark program. Notice that the 18-period moving average contributes as much to the solution as the SPY.

Another example of the effect of moving averages is presented in Appendix A as Case Study I. A 12-period moving average of each of the 6 inputs in the benchmark network are added to the network with great

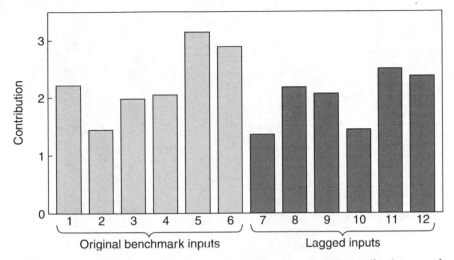

Figure 5–2 Adding lagged inputs to benchmark system. Contribution graph showing the effect of adding 5-period lagged inputs to original benchmark inputs (numbered 1–6). Note that lagged inputs (inputs 7–12) contribute to the solution almost as much as the original inputs. Input 7 is a lagged version of input 1, and so forth.

Contribution Graph

Contribution graphs show how much each input contributes to the network solution. It is done by adding the weights (strength of the connections) connected to any given input. Values greater than 5 are very strong and values from the 0 to 2 range are weak. These graphs are used extensively to evaluate inputs and to compare the results of preprocessing the data in various ways. It is a very powerful tool, because testing an idea this way is much more meaningful than using intuition. It also helps to identify inputs which are *colinear*. Colinear inputs are those that are very similar, but not exactly the same. For example, the Dow Jones Industrial Average is colinear with the S&P 500 which is colinear with the OEX. Use of colinear inputs harms more beginners networks than any other error, because the network is confused as to which of the colinear inputs is giving the *right* information.

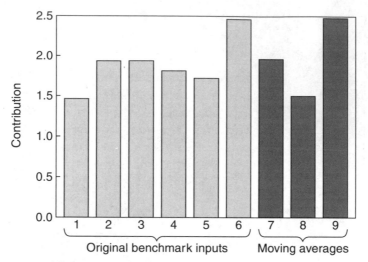

Figure 5–3   Adding moving averages. Contribution of original benchmark inputs (1–6) and moving averages of SPY (inputs 7–9). Moving average periods were 4, 9, 18 periods. Note that moving averages contribute as much to the solution as the original inputs.

improvement in the final results. To determine which moving average would have the most effect on the accuracy of the benchmark system, the network was run with the original 6 inputs plus the moving average of the 6 inputs (12 inputs total). The first test used a 1-period moving average (essentially the original data), and the second used a 2-period moving average. The following test used 3-, 4-, 5-, 8-, 10-, 12-, and 15-period moving averages. Figure 5–4 shows the result of that series of tests. A 12-period moving average was clearly the best.

In another test of the effects of moving averages, each of the 6 inputs were smoothed with a 15-day moving average, and these smoothed averages were used as the 6 inputs of the benchmark network. Figure 5–5 shows the contributions of each of these inputs. Notice that the 15-period moving of the TICK has now become the input contributing the most. When the data is used in its raw form (see Figure 4–2) the TICK is the third most important input, contributing about half of the SPY and XYX contribution.

Differences

Another preprocessing technique is the use of differences. For example, we can subtract today's value from the value 5 periods ago, 10

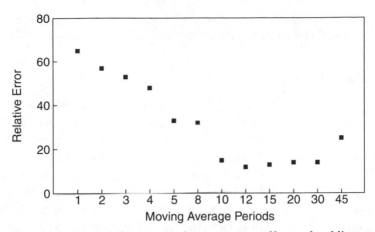

Figure 5–4   Locating optimum moving average. Effect of adding various moving averages to the network described in Appendix A. The sudden change in error between the 8 and 10-period moving average is real. The data was tested several times to establish that the discontinuity existed.

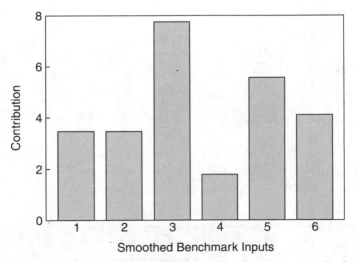

Figure 5–5   Effect of smoothing inputs. Benchmark inputs smoothed as a 15-period moving average. Compare to Figure 4–2 where the inputs are not smoothed.

periods ago, 15 periods ago, and 20 periods ago. Differences can also be considered the same as the technical indicator called *momentum*.

Normalizing Data

An excellent way to normalize data is to subtract today's value (or the value n-periods ago) from the current value of moving average. Figure 5–6 shows the original SPY data used in the benchmark network, and Figure 5–7 is the 50-day moving average of the data shown in Figure 5–6. Figure 5–8 is the result of subtracting the 50-day moving average from the original data.

Data can also be normalized using price relative to an index, change in price, percentage change in price, and ratios of two variables, which are covered in more detail in the next section.

Quotients

Dividing two variables can often make the data easier for the network to use. In addition, it reduces two inputs into one. To illustrate how this works, we deleted the ADV and DEC inputs from the benchmark network and replaced them by the quotient ADV/DEC. The new inputs

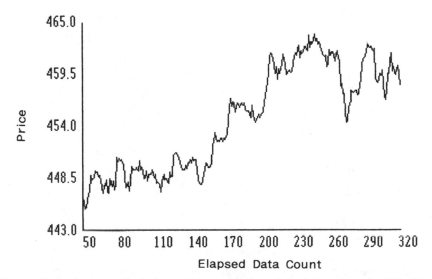

Figure 5–6 Unsmoothed data. Unsmoothed, original benchmark SPY data. Compare to Figure 5–7 which shows 50-day moving average of data.

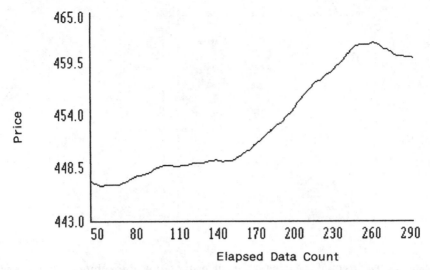

Figure 5–7 Smoothed data original benchmark SPY data smoothed with a 50-day moving average. Compare to Figure 4–7 which is the unsmoothed data.

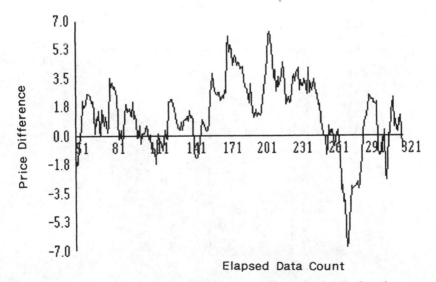

Figure 5–8 Effect of removing long-term trend. Original SPY data less a 50-day moving average (Figure 5–6 less Figure 5–7). This technique eliminates the longer term trend, and emphasizes the short time swings in the data.

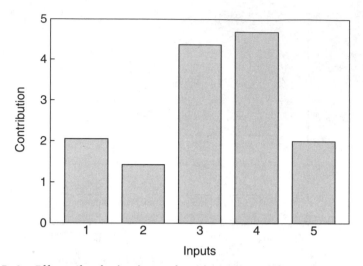

Figure 5–9 Effect of reducing inputs by using ratios of the inputs. Inputs ADV and DEC have been replaced by a single quotient of ADV/DEC. Inputs are TICK, TRIN, SPY, YXY and ADV/DEC. Compare to Figure 5–11.

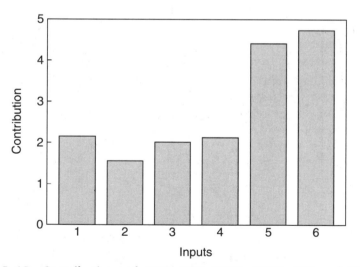

Figure 5–10 Contributions of ADV, DEC, TICK, TRIN, SPY and YXY for comparison with Figure 5–11.

are 1-TICK, 2-TRIN, 3-SPY, 4-YXY, and 5-ADV/DEC. The contribution of the new input ADV/DEC is shown in Figure 5–9. Figure 5–10 shows the contributions of the original benchmark network.

TECHNICAL STUDIES

Appendix B gives a list of the technical studies available in one neural software program. The constriction of most of these technical studies is beyond the scope of this book.

"IF-THEN-ELSE" RULES

Some neural network software programs contain a module called *If-Then-Else*. This module adds a column to the spreadsheet and

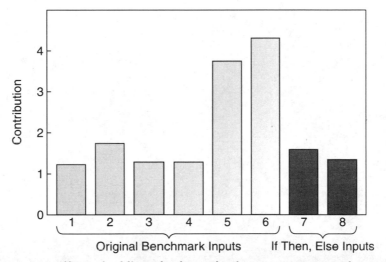

Figure 5–11 Effect of adding If, Then, Else inputs. Inputs 7 and 8 are the inputs resulting from using the If, Then, Else function. Notice how the addition of inputs 7 and 8 has reduced the contributions of the first four inputs. Compare this to Figure 5–10.

formulates different values according to the If-Then-Else statements. For example:

IF the 4-period moving average of SPY *is equal to or greater than* the 18-period moving average of SPY

THEN the column equals +1

ELSE the column equals 0

Figure 5–11 shows the contributions to the benchmark network of two If-Then-Else statements. The first is the one given in the previous example, and the second, similar to above except the first moving average is 9 periods.

6

OTHER WAYS TO
MANIPULATE DATA

This chapter could well be called "Tricks of the Trade" or possibly "House Keeping." It deals with fundamental phenomenoa, such as seasonality, that can be used to develop a better network. Repeated calendar events, or seasonality, can influence stock movements, forming patterns. This chapter addresses how to use these factors and how to incorporate man-made events into forecasts.

SEASONALITY

Some commodity and equity markets have a very strong seasonal component. This information can be communicated to the network by setting up a column in the spreadsheet called "seasonality." During the time of year when there is low price volatility, for example, for corn in the middle of winter, a zero (0) is entered in the column. During the summer, when prices vary greatly with each rain or rumor of drought, a plus one (+1) is entered in the column. In this way, the network is told whether to expect high or low volatility during these periods.

Daily and Monthly Identification

If we are designing a network to predict the number of bank tellers needed each day, the network needs a way to distinguish between the different days of the week. Tuesday is often the slowest day in the banking business, and Friday is the busiest day, with the other days ranked differently by region.

One way to handle this is by setting up columns for each day of the week. The days that are busiest are assigned a +1, those that are quiet get a 0. Using this technique, the network has a way to recognize the day of the week on which it is operating.

Another way for the network to recognize seasonality is to set up columns labeled with the months, or the four seasons, and then label the data as to which month or season it came from. Some neural network programs have modules that assist in accomplishing these labeling tasks.

MINIMUMS AND MAXIMUMS

Most software programs have some way of evaluating and establishing the maximums and minimums of the input and output data. If the data varies from 390 to 460 over the time span in question, it makes sense to limit the data range to 390 to 460 rather than 0 to 460, or 0 to 1000, for that matter. When the exact maximums and minimums are used, the network is tuned to 100 percent of the range of the data. If you were to use 0 to 460, the actual data would represent only about 18 percent of the total assigned range, and for 0 to 1000, the data range would represent only 5 percent of the expected range. Most neural network software programs will set the minimum and maximum values for all the inputs automatically. Restricting the range of maximums and minimums to the actual range gives the network more sensitivity to a change in value. A 1 point change is 0.1 percent when the range is 1000, and 1.4 percent when the range is 70. This differs by a factor of 14.

Outliers

An *outlier* is a value which is out of the normal range of the data, as shown in Figure 6–1. Most of the data in this figure is in the range of

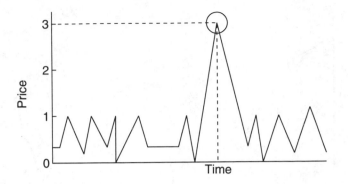

Figure 6–1 A data outlier where most of the data is between 0 and +1. Note outlier at time T and value 3. Copyright © 1990 Ward Systems Group.

0 to +1, except for the single value of +3 at time T. This point would be considered an outlier, because it is 3 times greater than any other value. Figure 6–2 shows the SPY data from the benchmark network. There are three possible outliers at periods 27, 46, and 265. Figure 6–3 is an enlargement of the periods from 0 to 56. Here the possible outliers at periods 27 and 46 can be more clearly seen.

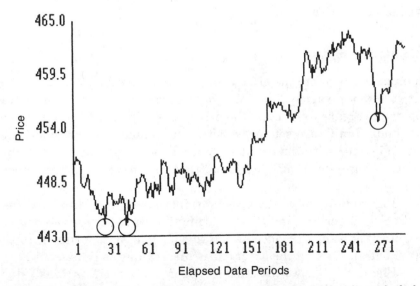

Figure 6–2 Outliers in the benchmark series. Note possible outliers circled at periods 27, 46, and 265.

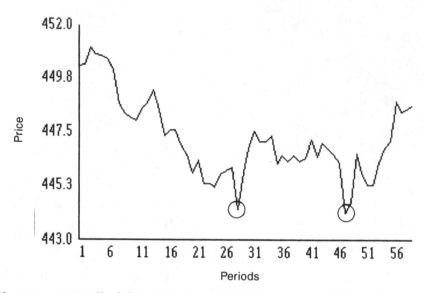

Figure 6–3   Detail of data items 1 to 56 of SPY. Note possible outliers at 27 and 46.

Outliers are affected by the choice of minimum and maximum settings. When the range is narrowed, some outliers are automatically eliminated, causing an increase in processing speed and change in the type of network solution.

Min/Max Examples

In order to illustrate the effects of Min/Max settings, we trained the network using various Min/Max values, ran new data, then plotted the error. Figure 6–4 shows the error curve when the minimum and maximum limits are set to the actual minimum and maximum values and tested with the test data that has been set aside. Notice that no error is greater that +/−2.5 and that the curve is centered about the 0 line.

Figure 6–5 shows the effects of increasing the Min/Max limit values by 40 percent and then reducing the range by 40 percent. Increasing the range produced a curve that is almost identical to the curve obtained using the actual Min/Max values as limits.

Figure 6–6 shows the effects of decreasing the Min/Max values by 40 percent. Here the error has climbed to +3.0 and −3.0 and the symmetry about the zero line has been lost.

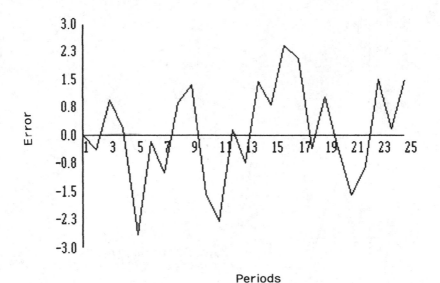

Figure 6–4   Error curve of benchmark system with MIN/MAX set to actual values of the minimums and maximums.

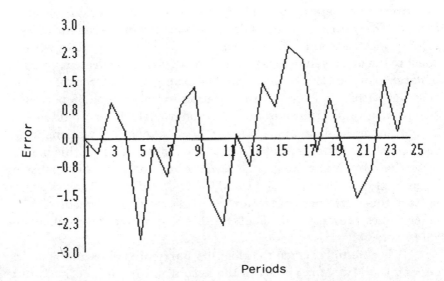

Figure 6–5   MIN/MAX set to value 40 percent greater than actual minimums and maximums.

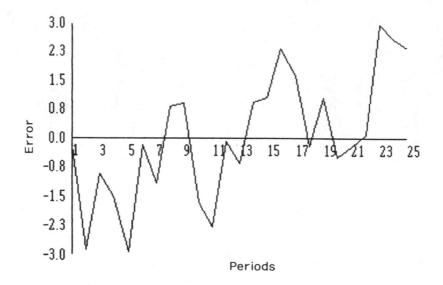

Figure 6–6 MIN/MAX reduced by 40 percent from the actual value of the minimums and maximums. Compare this to Figure 6–4.

Besides setting Min/Max values manually, automatically, and reducing or expanding the values by a set percent, some neural network programs allow determination by setting the value as a multiple of *one standard deviation* on either side of the mean value. A *standard deviation* is a statistical term indicating the distribution of data with respect to the mean value. Small standard deviations indicate a grouping of data clustered close to the mean. For example, 68 percent of all data that lies within $+/-1$ standard deviation would include 68 percent of the mean, a value of the mean $+/-2$ standard deviations would include 95 percent of the data, and a value of $+/-3$ standard deviations would include 99 percent of the data. To test the results of using this method of setting Min/Maxs, we set the standard deviation to 2.0, capturing 95 percent of the data, and repeated the test. Figure 6–7 shows the results of this test. These are by far the worst results obtained, with the error values ranging from about $+/-3.5$, and no symmetry about the zero line.

It is safe to conclude that for this particular data and network, setting the Min/Max values to the actual minimum and maximum values of the range gives the best results. In many cases, manually limiting the Min/Max values to less than 100 percent of the range or

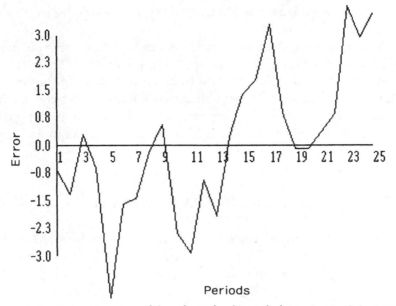

Figure 6–7   Error curve resulting from having Min/Max set to 2.0 standard deviations.

to a standard deviation factor so as to exclude outliers is necessary if the best possible network is to be developed. Run your own tests similar to the ones presented here to determine the best settings for the Min/Max function. Setting the minimum and maximum values too wide reduces the sensitivity of the network and includes outliers that confuse the network. Setting the values too narrow eliminates data that may have value to the network.

EXTRACTING TEST DATA

It is common practice to set aside part of the data in advance of training the network for the purpose of testing after training with data that has never been seen by the network. This is commonly called "out-of-sample testing." The most popular method for doing this is to take every tenth pattern or row and set it aside. Other methods randomly exclude 10 percent of the patterns, or simply save the last 10 percent of the file (the most recent data). There are valid arguments for each approach. Some even advocate extracting two data samples so they can be compared.

When running the benchmark system for illustrative purposes, every 10th pattern was set aside for testing purposes. The rationale for this was to *allow* the same data to be used for testing the network so that we could make a comparison between different benchmark networks. Normally, where comparisons are not necessary, the author would prefer a random extraction of 10 percent of the data for out-of-sample testing.

HOW MUCH DATA IS ENOUGH?

Most books and magazine articles state that each input should be supported by 10 rows of data (sometimes called *patterns* or *facts*). The benchmark system has only 6 inputs, so if this well-published rule is true, adding data beyond 60 patterns should not result in improved performance. However, examination of Figure 6–8 shows that network performance continues to improve as input data is added. R-squared was determined by using out-of-sample test data after training the network on the number of patterns shown along the X-axis. The number of inputs was 6. At the maximum number of available patterns (250), the input to pattern ratio is greater than 40 and was still showing improvement as more patterns were added. The

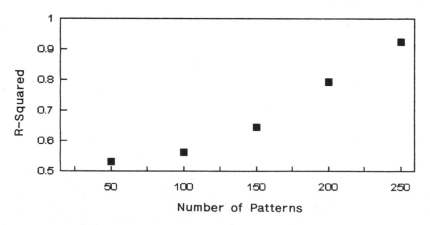

Figure 6–8 Shows improvement of R-squared as number of patterns is increased. Network had six inputs.

performance of this network would improve with the addition of more patterns. These results are consistent with the general statistical rule that *more data is better than less data*. Short cuts often lead to incomplete or erroneous results.

EFFECT OF NONTYPICAL EVENTS

1987 Crash and Persian Gulf War

The stock market crash of 1987 and the abrupt selloff of the market in August-October 1990 at the start of the Persian Gulf war are not typical events. If they were common and we had a few hundred of them on which to train, then neural networks might do a good job of forecasting when the next event would occur. However, since they occur so rarely and we cannot forecast a random occurrence, a decision must be made whether to include them in the data used for training a neural network. Excluding the effects of the Persian Gulf war still allows enough data for most applications.

However, a problem arises if weekly or monthly data is to be used. In the case of weekly data, there is only $\frac{1}{5}$ of the data available and for monthly studies, only $\frac{1}{22}$ values. This may not be enough for a statistically sound solution. One alternative is to try training both with and without the transient periods included in the data.

Early 1970s Data

It is generally agreed that the character of the stock market changed when option trading started in the early 1970s. This is another event which, as the crash of 1987 and Persian Gulf war, must be recognized and confronted. This event probably only affects network designers working with monthly data and those who make long-term forecasts.

7

TRAINING AND NETWORK ARCHITECTURES

This chapter covers the process of training and presents many of the training algorithms. In addition, it covers many of the neural network architectures.

TRAINING

Training is the process of teaching the network what we want it to learn. If we wanted to teach a person a set of facts, we might write the first fact (often called a "pattern") on a piece of paper and the next fact on another piece of paper, and so on, and then present the papers one at a time until the person had learned the facts or patterns. This technique is represented in Figure 7–1.

If we wanted an artificial neural network to simulate the human mind, we do the same thing, only in this case, we present the data from a spreadsheet, one row at a time. We can present the rows in either random order or in sequence one after another, a method called *rotation*. Certain neural network architectures require that the patterns must be presented in rotation; others will accept the data in either random fashion or in rotation.

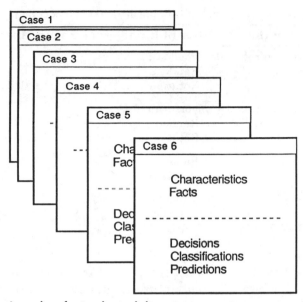

Figure 7–1 Learning facts—in training, we present one case after another until learning is accomplished. Used with permission of Ward Systems Group.

Training Algorithms

An *algorithm* is the name given to a method of training the network. The most common algorithm is the one called *momentum*. This algorithm can vary the learning rate or how fast a neural network learns. This algorithm can also vary the momentum of the learning rate. The momentum is the amount of the previous move that added to the present move. Most neural network software packages also contain other proprietary learning algorithms. These often are touted as having advantages in either accuracy, training speed, or other improved attributes.

To test how much the choice of training algorithm affected the results, the benchmark network was trained using various algorithms. The network architecture was a 3-layer back-propagation network and the measure of accuracy was the value of the minimum average error when tested with fresh data. The results of these tests are shown in Table 7–1.

It can be seen, using the benchmark data, that the selection of learning rate did not have a large effect, approximately +/−6%. In critical applications, the difference between 0.00456 and 0.00403

Table 7–1   Effect of training algorithm on accuracy.

Training Algorithm	Presentation	Minimum Average Error
Momentum (Learn rate 0.05, Momentum 0.5)		
	Random	0.00435
	Rotation	0.00417
Momentum (Learn rate 0.1, Momentum 0.1)		
	Random	0.00434
	Rotation	0.00403
Proprietary #1	Random	0.00434
	Rotation	0.00424
Proprietary #2	Random	NA
	Rotation	0.00456

could be the difference between success and failure. Once again, each application and network architecture should be tested with the various training algorithms to find the one that gives the best results.

NETWORK ARCHITECTURES

Although about 90 percent of all networks are of the 3-layer back-propagation type, there are many more, some very specialized. We will examine a number of architectures by training them using the benchmark data.

3-Layer Back-propagation Networks

When using the 3-layer back-propagation network, the two variables which must be fixed are the learning algorithm and the number of neurons in the hidden (second) layer (see Figure 7–2). The learning

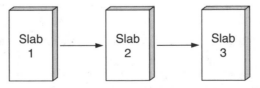

Figure 7–2   Schematic of 3-layer network. Slab 1 represents the input layer of neurons, slab 2 the hidden layer, and slab 3 the output layer.

Table 7–2   Effect of number of hidden neurons on accuracy.

Number of Neurons in Hidden Layer	Minimum Average Error
One (*Yes, one*)	0.00446
Two	0.00441
Three	0.00425
Four	0.00433
Five	0.00440
Seven	0.00435
Ten	0.00430
Fifteen	0.00431
Twenty	0.00426
Thirty	0.00425
Forty	0.00426

algorithm variables were discussed earlier in the chapter, under the section titled Training Algorithms.

We investigated the effect of varying the number of neurons in the hidden layer by training the network with between 1 and 40 neurons in the hidden layer. The benchmark data was used and the valuation was the average minimum error of 31 (new) test data patterns. A momentum algorithm with a learning rate of 0.05 and a momentum factor of 0.5 was used. The results are shown in Table 7–2.

Notice in Table 7–2 that the error varies by only 5 percent and even the network with only *one* hidden neuron was within 5 percent of the best network. Different neural network practitioners have suggested alternate formulas for determining the number of neurons in the hidden layer. The most common one is to start with the number of hidden neurons being equal to the total of the inputs and outputs. In the case above, that would have resulted in seven hidden neurons. Using this formula would have resulted in about an average network.

The number of hidden neurons does not seem to be a critical area, and tests such as this one can result in finding the optimum number of hidden neurons. Figure 7–3 presents the data of Figure 7–2 in graphical form.

4-Layer Networks

Four-layer networks are like 3-layer networks, except an extra layer is inserted between the hidden layer and the output layer, as shown in

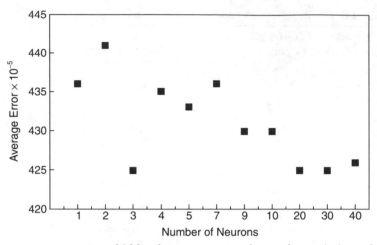

Figure 7–3 **Error verses hidden-layer neurons. Shows the variation of error with number of neurons in hidden layer.**

Figure 7–4. Several researchers working with serial data have reported slight improvements when a fourth layer is added with the number of neurons being 10 percent of the total of the number of neurons in the hidden and output layers. To determine if that was true with our benchmark data, we added a fourth layer to a network having a second layer of three neurons and a network having 30 neurons. The result of that series of tests is shown in Table 7–3.

From this data on network configurations, we conclude that the results are no better than those obtained with the standard, straight out of the box, 3-layer back-propagation network.

Although it is possible to construct 5-layer networks, no tests were run on this configuration. The number of variables would require an enormous amount of testing.

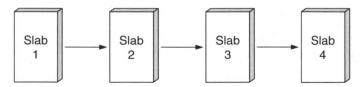

Figure 7–4 **Schematic of a 4-layer network. Slabs 2 and 3 are the hidden layers.**

Table 7–3   Effect of adding second hidden layer on accuracy.

Network Architecture			Average Error
Input layer	Hidden layer 1	Hidden layer 2	
6	3	3	0.00449
6	3	2	0.00458
6	30	30	0.00432
6	30	15	0.00430
6	30	7	0.00438
6	30	3	0.00454

Recurrent Networks

Recurrent networks, also known as *Jordan Elman networks,* have the ability to remember patterns. Typical patterns might be a "double bottom" or a "head-and-shoulders top." They are often used in financial networks with excellent results. Recurrent networks have one liability: They take a long time to train. This is not a problem with a relatively small network and small data field such as we use with the benchmark data, but it is when the number of inputs and rows of data grow from the benchmark's 6 inputs to 25 and the rows of data go from the 327 of the benchmark system to 900. The benchmark data trains in under three minutes with 3-layer networks; it took about 30 minutes to train each of the three recurrent networks. These run times were obtained using a computer with a 486DX-33 processor.

Recurrent networks are similar to 3-layer back-propagation networks except they have a fourth group of neurons to which connections are made from the other three groups of neurons. These groups of neurons are called slabs (see Figure 7–4). In a 3-layer back-propagation network, there are only three slabs: the input layer would be slab one, the hidden layer slab two, and the output layer slab three.

There are three types of recurrent networks distinguished by how the fourth slab gets its feedback (input from one of the other three layers or slabs). The first type gets feedback from the input layer as in Figure 7–5, the second from the hidden layer (see Figure 7–6), and the last gets feedback from the output (see Figure 7–7).

To determine whether recurrent networks result in better accuracy when used with the benchmark data, the data was run with each of the three types of recurrent networks. The number of neurons in each slab (layer) was determined by accepting the default value of the neural network software package used. For the network with feedback

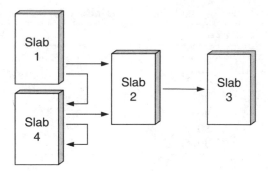

Figure 7–5   Recurrent network with feedback from the input layer (slab 1) to the recurrent layer (slab 4).

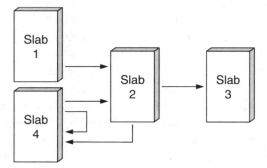

Figure 7–6   Recurrent network with feedback from hidden layer (slab 2) to the recurrent layer (slab 4).

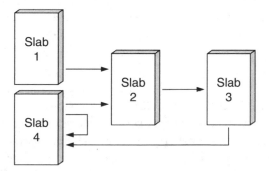

Figure 7–7   Recurrent network with feedback from output layer (slab 3) to recurrent layer (slab 4).

from the input layer, the numbers were as follows: input layer (slab 1) 6 neurons, hidden layer (slab 2) was 20 neurons, output layer (slab 3) 1, and the recurrent slab (slab 4) was 6. For the network with feedback from the hidden layer, the number of neurons in the recurrent slab were 20. For the network with feedback from the output, the number of neurons in the recurrent slab were 6.

Recurrent Network Type	Minimum Average Error
Feedback from input layer	0.00440
Feedback from hidden layer	0.00385
Feedback from output layer	0.00402

The recurrent networks with feedback from the output layer and hidden layer did better than any of the 3-layer or 4-layer networks, tested previously.

Jump Connection Networks

A *jump connection network* is a type of back-propagation network in which every layer is connected or linked to every previous layer. When the hidden layers are increased beyond one layer, the training time is usually increased.

The 3-Layer Jump Connection Network. A 3-layer jump connection network (see Figure 7–8) was tested with the benchmark data. The results showed an minimum average error of 0.000481.

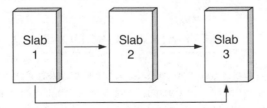

Figure 7–8 A 3-layer jump connection network.

The 4-Layer Jump Connection Network. The schematic diagram for the 4-layer jump connection network is shown in Figure 7–9. This network tested badly with a minimum average error of 0.00544.

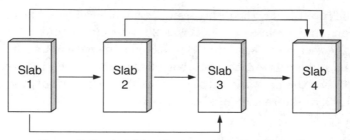

Figure 7–9   A 4-layer jump connection network.

5-Layer Jump Connection Network.   Figure 7–10 shows the connections for a 5-layer jump connection network. This was the worst performer yet, with a minimum average error of 0.00633 when trained and tested with the benchmark data.

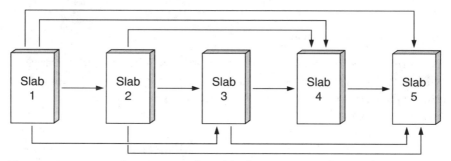

Figure 7–10   A 5-layer network with jump connections. This network performed very poorly when tested with the benchmark data.

ACTIVATION FUNCTIONS

Activation functions are the mathematical transfer functions that determine which level of the data is given the most emphasis. For example, if a linear function is used, all the data is treated equally (see Figure 7–11). A Tanh function (hyperbolic tangent) gives much more emphasis to the information around 0 and very little emphasis to values around $+1$ and -1 (see Figure 7–13).

The mathematical formulas for the various activation functions are as follows:

Logistic	$f(x) = 1/(1+\exp(-x))$
Linear	$f(x) = x$
Tanh	$f(x) = \tanh(x)$
Tanh15	$f(x) = \tanh(1.5x)$
Sine	$f(x) = \text{sine}(x)$
Symmetric logistic	$f(x) = 2/(1 + \exp(-x))-1$
Gaussian	$f(x) = \exp(-x^2)$
Gaussian complement	$f(x) = 1 - \exp(-x^2)$

The graphs of these functions are shown in Figures 7–11 through 7–18.

Most neural network programs use the logistic function unless another function is specifically chosen by the user. Some neural network programs allow choosing different activation functions. The 3-layer back-propagation network was trained with the different activation functions with these results:

Activation Function	Minimum Average Error
Logistic	0.00403
Linear	0.00416
Tanh	0.00394
Gaussian	0.00400
Sine	0.00396
Tanh15	0.00394
Symmetric logistic	0.00397
Gaussian complement	0.00387

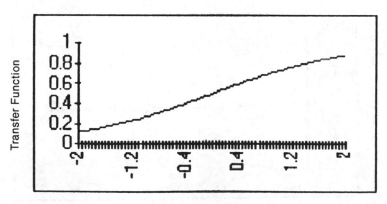

Logistic

Figure 7–11   Logistic activation function.

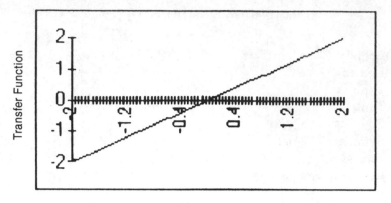

Linear

Figure 7–12   Linear activation function.

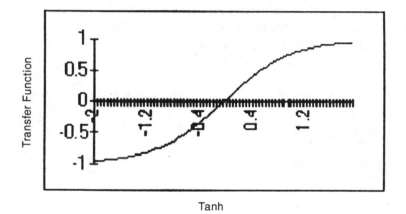

Tanh

Figure 7–13   Tanh activation function.

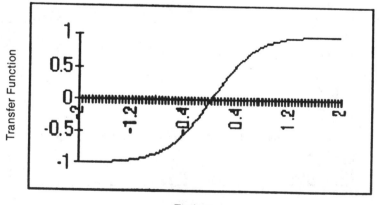

Tanh15

Figure 7–14   Tanh15 activation function.

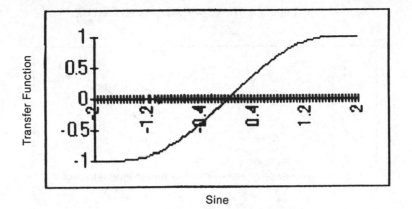

Figure 7–15   Sine activation function.

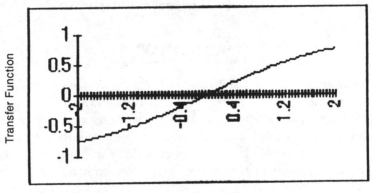

Figure 7–16   Symmetric logistic activation function.

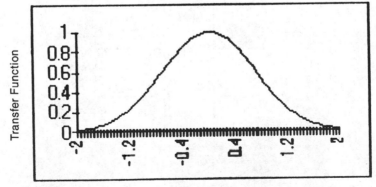

Figure 7–17   Gaussian activation function.

81

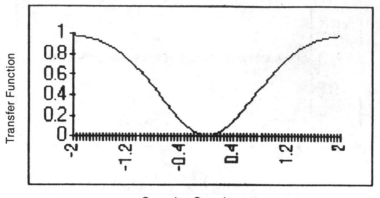

Gaussian Complement

Figure 7–18 Gaussian-complement activation function.

WARD NETWORKS

Ward networks use extra slabs each of which can have different activation functions. For example, the Ward net shown in Figure 7–19 is similar to a standard 3-layer network, except an extra slab (slab 3) of neurons is in parallel with the normal hidden layer (slab 2). Thus, this network has two hidden layers, each of which can have a different activation function. For testing purposes, the network was trained using

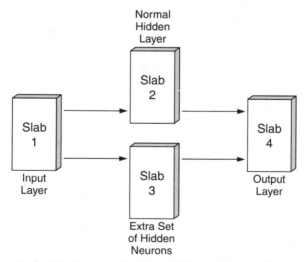

Figure 7–19 Basic Ward network. Two hidden slabs, each with a different activation function.

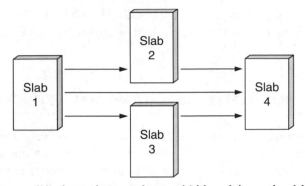

Figure 7–20   Modified Ward network. Two hidden slabs each with a different activation function and a jump connection, allowing slab 1 to go directly to slab 4.

the benchmark data with one slab having a Gaussian activation function and the other having a Gaussian-complement. A minimum average error of 0.00431 was obtained. The training algorithm was momentum with the learning rate set to 0.05 and the momentum set at 0.5.

The network shown in Figure 7–20 had an added jump connection allowing the input slab (slab 1) to go directly to the output (slab 4), and use the same Gaussian and Gaussian-Complement activation functions as above, and when trained had a minimum average error of 0.00395.

The network of Figure 7–21 which has three hidden layers in parallel was also trained. In addition to the Gaussian and Gaussian-

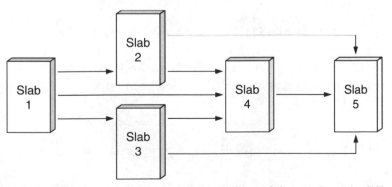

Figure 7–21   Ward network having three hidden slabs, each with different activation functions.

complement activation functions, the third slab had a tanh activation function. The trained network had a minimum average error of 0.00403.

KOHONEN SELF-ORGANIZING MAP NETWORKS

The purpose of *Kohonen networks* is to separate outputs into categories. For example, using real estate data similar to that described in Chapter 4, a Kohonen network could be used to classify data into high, medium, and low priced homes. Kohonen networks are *unsupervised,* that is, they have no output value in the training pattern to which training can be compared.

Kohonen networks have two layers (see Figure 7–22), the input layer of N variables and an output layer, which has one output for each category. During training, the patterns are presented in either rotational or random sequence to the network, then propagated to the output layer and evaluated. This process is repeated for the number of epochs chosen in advance.

The network is very sensitive to learning rate, and the better software programs slowly reduce the learning rate as training progresses. The network adjusts the weights to the output neurons in a *neighborhood* around the neuron. The neighborhood size is variable; it begins large and slowly reduces to zero. Kohonen networks work by clustering patterns based on their distance from each other. The benchmark data was not tested with the Kohonen network since the Kohonen network is not used with series data.

PROBABILISTIC NEURAL NETWORKS (PNN)

Probabilistic Neural Networks (PNN) separate data into a specified number of output categories. PNN networks are known for their ability

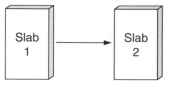

Figure 7–22   Schematic representation of and unsupervised (Kohonen) neural network.

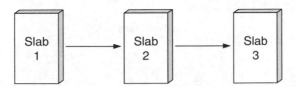

Figure 7–23   Schematic representation of Probabilistic Neural Network.

to train rapidly on sparse data sets. PNN networks are 3-layer networks as seen in Figure 7–23). The number of output neurons is determined by the number of categories. The number of hidden neurons is equal to the number of training patterns.

Both PNN networks and General Regression Neural Networks (GRNN) require that a smoothing factor be used when applying the network.

Smoothing Factors

PNN and GRNN networks require the application of a smoothing factor. In Figures 7–24 through 7–26, output patterns 25, 50 and 75 have a value of +1; all other values are zero. In Figure 7–24, a smoothing factor of 0.05 is used and the values are close to +1 and 0. When the smoothing factor is raised to 0.08 (as shown in Figure 7–25) the values are in a range of 0.5 to 1. When the smoothing factor is raised to 0.1 (as in Figure 7–26) all the values are close to 1 and the differences between values are "smoothed" or topped off. The benchmark data was not applied to the PNN networks since the network, like the Kohonen network, is intended for classifying.

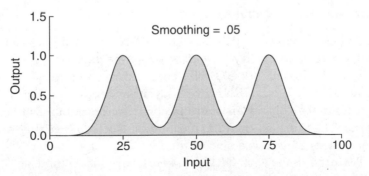

Figure 7–24   Output verses input with smoothing factor of 0.05. Compare to Figures 7–25 and 7–26.

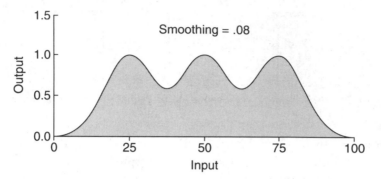

Figure 7–25   Output verses input with a smoothing factor of 0.08. Compare to Figures 7–24 and 7–26.

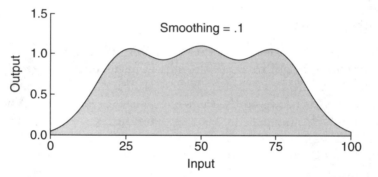

Figure 7–26   Output verses input with a smoothing factor of 0.1. Compare to Figures 7–24 and 7–25.

General Regression Neural Networks (GRNN)

General Regression Neural Networks (GRNN), as with PNN networks, are known for their ability to work with sparse data sets. Rather than classify as PNN networks, GRNN networks are able to produce continuous value outputs. GRNN are 3-layer networks (see Figure 7–27), with the number of hidden neurons equal to the number of training patterns. There are no training parameters such as learning rate and momentum, but there is a smoothing factor.

Training times with GRNN networks are fast compared to back-propagation networks, and very fast when compared to recurrent

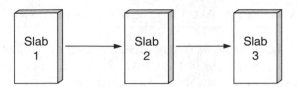

Figure 7–27 Schematic representation of a General Regression Neural Network (GRNN).

networks. Using the benchmark data to train a GRNN network, the results were a disappointing 0.00634. However, when a 12-period moving average of each of the inputs was added, the minimum average error became 0.00115 almost 4 times better that the best recurrent network (see Appendix A). This shows the value of preprocessing as well as the ability of GRNN network to deal with series data. GRNN networks, when given properly preprocessed data, outperform most, if not all, other network architectures when used with serial data.

Figure 7–28 shows the error of a GRNN network as it trains. Notice that the network tries different smoothing factors until it reaches a minimum error. The benchmark network trained in about 1 minute 30 seconds on a computer using a 486DX33 processor. This compares with about 30 minutes when the benchmark data was trained on a recurrent network.

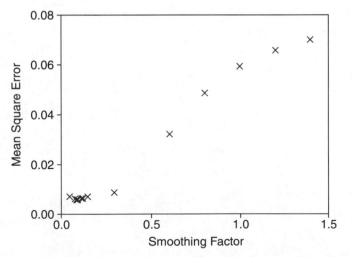

Figure 7–28 Plot of error of a network verses the smoothing factor.

GENETIC-ADAPTIVE GRNN NETWORKS

In mid-1994, Ward Systems Group introduced a new type of GRNN network, called a *Genetic-Adaptive GRNN Network*. These networks differ from conventional GRNN networks in that they have a number of smoothing factors, one for each input plus a conventional overall smoothing factor. In essence, during training the smoothing factor for each input plus the overall smoothing factor are adjusted to obtain the lowest error wher tested with the test data. The new Ward Systems network is said to be about twice as accurate as the GRNN network. This claim appears to be true, based on the preliminary tests. This network, when tested on time-series data gives the best results of all the networks and algorithms tested so far.

The downside to these networks is that the training time is very long. Where a regular GRNN network would train in two minutes, a Genetic-Adaptive GRNN might take one hour.

8

LESSONS IN STARTING AND STOPPING TRAINING

This chapter covers starting and stopping training, and suggestions about what to try if the network won't train, and applying (using) the network.

STARTING THE TRAINING

After collecting data, importing it into a spreadsheet, preprocessing, setting minimums and maximums, separating out data for testing the network, choosing a network architecture and training algorithm, starting training is the easiest part of the whole process. For neural network programs that run under the DOS operating system, rather than Windows or OS/2, a 2-key command such as "control T" gets training started; in Windows programs, a double click on a special icon gets training started.

As explained in Chapter 7, training is the repetitive presentation of the data (in patterns or rows) to the network in hope that the network will be able to find the interrelationships between the various inputs. Figures 8–1 through 8–4 show the progress of a 3-layer network as it learns the training set derived from the benchmark data. The momentum training algorithm used a learn rate of 0.05

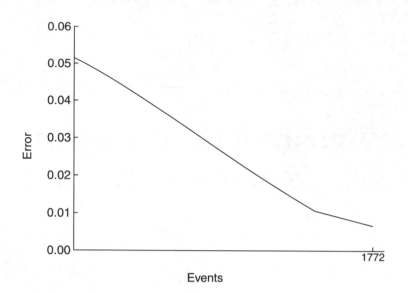

Figure 8–1   Error verses training time. This graph shows the error of the test set as training progresses. 1,772 learning events have taken place and the rate of training is beginning to slow down.

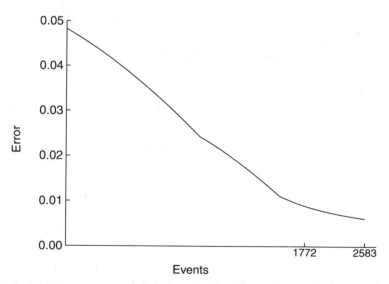

Figure 8–2   Error verses training time. This graph is the same as that shown in Figure 9–1 except the training has been extended to 2,583 events. Notice that the rate of training is slowed even further.

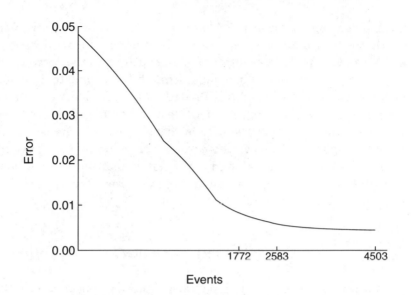

Figure 8–3   Error verses training time. Here the training has been extended to 4,503 training events. Training rate is further slowed.

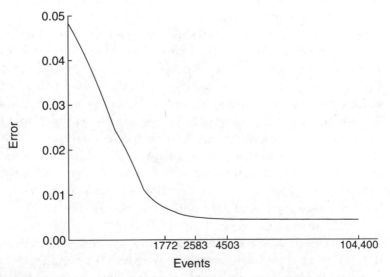

Figure 8–4   The training has been extended to 104,400 training events. Learning is very slow, but the network appears to be still learning after all this time.

and a momentum factor of 0.5. The vertical axis is the error of the network, the horizontal axis represents the number of learning events (a learning event is the presentation of one pattern to the network; an epoch is the presentation of one pass through the complete data set). Figure 8–1 shows the state of affairs after only 1,772 learning events. Figure 8–2 shows the progress a little further along, after 2,583 learning events. Note that the rate of learning slows between 1,772 and 2,583. Figure 8–3 shows the error after 4,305 learning events. Note that the learning has slowed appreciably and that there is some hunting for a solution. Figure 8–4 shows the error curve after learning has stopped at 104,400 learning events.

STOPPING THE TRAINING

When training back-propagation networks, there is a best point in the training process. As the set of graphs (Figures 8–1 through 8–4) show, as training starts learning is very quick. As training progresses, the rate of learning decreases (the slope of the curve becomes flatter). Finally, learning stops and memorization begins. The problem with *memorization* is that although it may help the network when it is dealing with the training data, it leads to poor results when presented with fresh, out-of-sample test data.

Figure 8–5, which is a magnification of the right part of the curve shown in Figure 8–4, presents the error curve of the test data late in the training process and it shows this effect very clearly. Note that the learning process proceeds as expected up to the point of the vertical arrow. Here the learning process degrades. This is because the network is now memorizing the training data rather than learning it, and thus the network begins to preform less well on the test data.

The objective is to stop the training at the point where memorization begins. Several neural network software programs have the ability to stop the training process, test the network with the test data, and save this network if, and only if, the test result is better than previous tests. If the results are not better than previous tests, the network is not saved. After testing, the network continues training. Usually, training is stopped for testing with the test data every 50 to 200 learning events. More frequent testing results in more accurate networks at the expense of training time. A compromise solution is to test every 200 events during the early stages of training and every 50

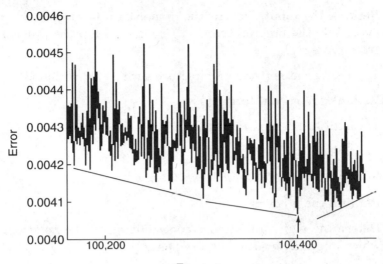

Events

Figure 8-5   This is a magnification of the end of the curve shown in Figure 8-4. Notice that the network is not able to improve on the performance that occurred at the arrow. Normally, if the network cannot improve after 10,000 events, it is considered trained.

events as memorization is approached (when improvement slows). It is normal to continue training the network for 10,000 to 20,000 learning events after the "best" network in order to determine that further training will not improve results.

If the software program being used does not have automatic determination of the "best" network as described above, then the process of stopping training and testing the network with the test data must be done manually.

TRAINING TO THE CORRECT ACCURACY LEVEL

Occasionally a set of data will not train to the accuracy level needed by the user. Some options that can be tried are:

1. Rethink the output target. Are you trying to be too accurate?

2. Add or subtract neurons in the hidden layer.

3. Rethink the inputs. Is this the proper data to forecast your objective? Is the preprocessing sufficient to allow the program to train properly?

4. Try a different network architecture such as recurrent or GRNN.

5. Rethink the output target.

6. Try a different learning algorithm.

7. Rethink the inputs.

8. Add or subtract hidden layers.

9. Rethink the problem.

10. Determine which inputs are contributing to the solution and which might be holding training back.

11. Tighten or loosen the min/max limits.

12. Change the forecast goal. For example, forecast the change in S&P rather than the absolute value.

13. In forecasting only one output, multiply that output by -1 and then forecast both outputs, the real one and the one multiplied by -1. Sometimes, when the network has to work harder, it comes up with more accurate answers. If these two outputs do not have very similar absolute values, something is wrong with the network.

14. Rethink the output, inputs, problem, architecture, learning algorithm, minimums and maximums, and preprocessing.

USING THE NETWORK

To use the network, most neural network software programs require that the new data must be put into a spreadsheet. Sometimes, the new data is an additional row added at the bottom of the spreadsheet file. Sometimes, a separate file is established.

When entering new data to use with the network, it is important that the data appear in the proper columns. Most neural network files have, in addition to the active columns, a lot of columns which contain data which has never been exposed to the network (for example date information). It is necessary to make sure that the new data is not put into these columns in error.

Because recurrent networks can remember patterns in the data, they require not only the new data, but the data from 10 or 20 periods ago. For example, a trained recurrent network might be able to recognize a double bottom or top pattern. Since these patterns take some period of time to develop, it is necessary that the recurrent network be presented with sufficient data to recognize the pattern.

Once the new data has been entered into the appropriate spreadsheet file, either as an addition to an existing file or as a new file, that file is called up by the network and the network is "run." After running, the data is examined to see what result has been forecast. While running the network is comparatively quick and easy, collecting the necessary data is sometimes a relatively lengthy task. This is typically the biggest complaint about the daily use of neural networks.

9

DEVELOPING A NETWORK TO FORECAST THE S&P 500 TEN DAYS INTO THE FUTURE

The primary objective of this chapter is to develop a network to forecast the S&P 500 10 days into the future. The 10-day forecast gives relatively long-term information on how the market is likely to behave.

A second objective is to develop a network that uses as few inputs as possible and still achieves the desired accuracy. Too many inputs make the network hard to use and allows a greater chance of overfitting. Handling of large amounts of data also increases the chance of mistakes. Often nonprofessionals are frustrated and stop using their networks because of the sheer amount of work required to collect, process, and apply the input data during daily operation. A network with the minimum number of inputs which meets the accuracy requirements is much more likely to be used daily.

The path followed to obtain the finished network is only one of millions of possible approaches. What is most significant is the total approach, the logic behind the various decisions, the method of resolving problems, the paths followed at decision points versus the paths ignored, and the reason for these decisions. Each network designer has particular prejudices and preconceptions which will affect the work. Each designer uses the same data in entirely different fashion with better or worse performance. It is the final forecasting accuracy that determines the success of the effort.

In setting out to write this chapter, we rejected using hindsight to make the progress from beginning to end appear seamless. Although that would have been illustrative of the process, it would not have stressed the reality of modeling. We learn more from the frequent dead ends that occur during the preprocessing stage. Therefore, we have shown the false starts and the trial-and-error process to provide a practical example of the development of a neural network.

THE INITIAL INPUTS

The following 13 inputs were downloaded from the Dial Data vendor:

Oil Index (XOI)
Dow Jones Industrial Average (DOW-30)
Dow Jones Transportation Average
Dow Jones Utility Average
S&P 500 Index
CRB Index
US Dollar Index
3-Month Treasury Bill Interest Rate
1-Year Treasury Bill Interest Rate
Gold and Silver Mining Index
S&P 100 (OEX)
Advance-Decline Index
TRIN

COLLECTING THE DATA

Although occasionally data is manually entered into a computer file, the most common way to collect data is through a modem that will access a data vendor and allow automatic updating of prices and statistics. For this project, the downloading was done using Equis Down Loader® software and saved in a Metastock® file. The data format was Compu-Trac®/Metastock. The period covered was March 1, 1991, to April 25, 1994, more than 800 days of data. Data earlier than March 1, 1991 was intentionally omitted because of the violent shifts in the market from August 1, 1990 through late February 1991, the result of the Persian Gulf War. These violent shifts are not typical of the market either before or after the war; therefore, it is appropriate to eliminate this period for training the network.

PROCESSING THE DATA

Each one of the 13 files was accessed sequentially in Equis Metastock® (MS). Each file was printed to a text file, and automatically saved in the MS directory. The MS text files were then imported into Lotus 1,2,3® as 13 separate text files. Figure 9–1 shows the DOW-30 text file after being imported into Lotus. This file was then *parsed,* a technique that is available in most spreadsheets, to convert text files to data files with all the data arranged in separate columns. In text files, the columns are not delineated. Notice that parsing converts the date file from the American format of month-day-year to the number of the day in this century.

Figure 9–2 shows the same file after parsing and replacing of the original test file. Labels have been added. The final data for the DOW-30 file consists of columns giving the date, the high, low, and closing price information, and the volume. Note that the date is given as the day of the century. It is very important that the date information be saved at this point. Later, most of the date information will be erased, but until then the date information must be saved as part of the file.

After all 13 files have been parsed, the high and low were erased except for the S&P 500. Except for Dow 30, all volume information was also erased. Thus with the exception of the S&P 500, all the files were "close only" files and contained no high or low information. However, the Dow 30 file contained volume data as well as the close, high, low information.

When all the parsing and deletion of excess information had been accomplished, the files were brought into one large spreadsheet by using the Lotus *File Combine* command. When forecast targets, lags, and moving averages are introduced, the number of rows available for training and testing will shrink by about 40 lines. Figure 9–3 (on pp. 102–103) shows the combined files before the date columns were deleted.

It is at this point that the data is examined to be sure that all the date columns are aligned. We can not stress enough the importance of this step. In this case, the following columns lacked date integrity: 3-month Treasury bills, 1-year Treasury bills, Dollar Index,

MetaStock

Price and Indicator Data
03/01/91 to 07/22/94

Security: DOW JONES IND 30   Indicator: NONE

Date	High	Low	Close	Volume Indicator Last M.A.
03/01/91	2923.51	2846.78	2909.90	272470
03/04/91	2950.74	2897.03	2914.11	214530
03/05/91	2995.54	2913.86	2972.52	283650
03/06/91	3017.82	2957.67	2973.27	312750
03/07/91	2998.51	2948.51	2963.37	212890
03/08/91	3003.47	2934.90	2955.20	243280
03/11/91	2975.50	2923.27	2939.36	165280
03/12/91	2962.13	2906.68	2922.52	182990
03/13/91	2967.82	2910.89	2955.20	190200
03/14/91	3000.00	2925.74	2952.23	250040
03/15/91	2966.58	2918.81	2948.27	383820
03/18/91	2960.64	2899.75	2929.95	170370
03/19/91	2908.17	2840.84	2867.82	252890
03/20/91	2897.03	2840.84	2872.03	257190
03/21/91	2907.92	2841.58	2855.45	237240
03/22/91	2879.95	2829.21	2858.91	174330
03/25/91	2897.52	2837.87	2865.84	167890
03/26/91	2924.01	2848.02	2914.85	256330
03/27/91	2956.93	2886.14	2917.57	252850
03/28/91	2942.08	2893.32	2913.86	178990
04/01/91	2919.31	2868.32	2881.19	162160
04/02/91	2951.98	2878.22	2945.05	210660
04/03/91	2970.54	2915.84	2926.73	206520
04/04/91	2959.41	2899.75	2924.50	221630
04/05/91	2949.26	2876.98	2896.78	201700
04/08/91	2929.21	2877.72	2918.56	139630
04/09/91	2932.43	2863.37	2873.02	173840
04/10/91	2902.48	2848.51	2874.50	170130
04/11/91	2937.62	2877.72	2905.45	239430
04/12/91	2946.53	2884.16	2920.79	229420
04/15/91	2957.18	2896.29	2933.17	218910
04/16/91	2995.79	2912.13	2986.88	257900
04/17/91	3030.45	2963.12	3004.46	327500
04/18/91	3027.72	2976.24	2999.26	252520
04/19/91	3000.25	2943.56	2965.59	237760
04/22/91	2962.13	2911.63	2927.72	211280
04/23/91	2957.92	2905.94	2930.45	185520
04/24/91	2965.10	2913.37	2949.51	202080

Figure 9–1   Metastock text file of Dow-30 imported into Lotus 1, 2, 3.

DATE	HIGH	LOW	CLOSE	VOLUME
33298	2923.51	2846.78	2909.9	272470
33301	2950.74	2897.03	2914.11	214530
33302	2995.54	2913.86	2972.52	283650
33303	3017.82	2957.67	2973.27	312750
33304	2998.51	2948.51	2963.37	212890
33305	3003.47	2934.9	2955.2	243280
33308	2975.5	2923.27	2939.36	165280
33309	2962.13	2906.68	2922.52	182990
33310	2967.82	2910.89	2955.2	190200
33311	3000	2925.74	2952.23	250040
33312	2966.58	2918.81	2948.27	383820
33315	2960.64	2899.75	2929.95	170370
33316	2908.17	2840.84	2867.82	252890
33317	2897.03	2840.84	2872.03	257190
33318	2907.92	2841.58	2855.45	237240
33319	2879.95	2829.21	2858.91	174330
33322	2897.52	2837.87	2865.84	167890
33323	2924.01	2848.02	2914.85	256330
33324	2956.93	2886.14	2917.57	252850
33325	2942.08	2893.32	2913.86	178990
33329	2919.31	2868.32	2881.19	162160
33330	2951.98	2878.22	2945.05	210660
33331	2970.54	2915.84	2926.73	206520
33332	2959.41	2899.75	2924.5	221630
33333	2949.26	2876.98	2896.78	201700
33336	2929.21	2877.72	2918.56	139630
33337	2932.43	2863.37	2873.02	173840
33338	2902.48	2848.51	2874.5	170130
33339	2937.62	2877.72	2905.45	239430
33340	2946.53	2884.16	2920.79	229420
33343	2957.18	2896.29	2933.17	218910
33344	2995.79	2912.13	2986.88	257900
33345	3030.45	2963.12	3004.46	327500
33346	3027.72	2976.24	2999.26	252520
33347	3000.25	2943.56	2965.59	237760
33350	2962.13	2911.63	2927.72	211280
33351	2957.92	2905.94	2930.45	185520
33352	2965.1	2913.37	2949.51	202080
33353	2958.42	2905.2	2921.04	174770
33354	2934.9	2888.61	2912.38	173310
33357	2941.09	2869.55	2876.98	163820
33358	2929.21	2859.41	2887.87	266030
33359	2945.3	2882.43	2930.2	215330
33360	2966.34	2917.33	2938.61	182340
33361	2959.9	2906.93	2938.86	171260
33364	2956.84	2911.45	2941.64	151990

Figure 9–2   Dow-30 text file after parsing and deletion of the original text file. Notice that dates have been converted to days of the century.

and ADV/DEC. Since we had a large amount of data, the columns lacking data integrity were deleted. Another way to handle this problem would be to locate the place where there is missing data and substitute an average of the values on either side of the missing data.

After date integrity has been established, all of the date columns except one are deleted. One column of date information is kept so that additional data can be added to the network at some future time if required. Figure 9–4 (on pp. 102–103) shows 22 rows of the finished spreadsheet. At this point, we have the following inputs:

S&P 500 (High, Low, and Close)
Oil Index
Dow Jones Industrial Average
Volume of Dow Jones Industrial Average
Dow Jones Utilities Index
Dow Jones Transportation Index
CRB Index
Gold and Silver Mining Index
OEX
TRIN

DETERMINING WHICH
INPUTS ARE MAKING CONTRIBUTIONS

To find out which inputs were making the most significant contributions, a 3-layer back-propagation network using a momentum algorithm having a training rate of 0.05 and a momentum of 0.5 was trained using the inputs. Table 9–1 shows the ranked performance of the 10 inputs. The minimum and maximum values of the inputs were set to the actual minimum and maximum values. Every tenth pattern was saved to a test file, a total of 78 patterns to be used for out-of-sample evaluation. There were 688 training patterns.

After 300,200 events the network was trained. That is, further training did not result in improved performance when tested with the out-of-sample data. When tested with the out-of-sample data, the network had an R-squared of 0.9549. Table 9–1 shows the contributions of the various inputs. The best inputs are at the bottom of the list, and the weaker inputs at the top. Figure 9–5 shows the contributions as a bar chart.

DATE	S&P-HIGH	S&P-LOW		S&P-CLOS		OIL		CRB
33343	361.67	358.01	33343	360.48	33343	256.49	33343	220.58
33344	366.75	358.96	33344	366.75	33344	258.68	33344	220.57
33345	370.1	366.04	33345	368.67	33345	259.86	33345	220.16
33346	370.01	367.09	33346	367.85	33346	258.39	33346	218.04
33347	367.86	363.67	33347	365.1	33347	256.63	33347	217.72
33350	365.1	360.49	33350	361.51	33350	254.98	33350	217.79
33351	363.89	359.5	33351	361.35	33351	257.71	33351	217.95
33352	363.18	359.96	33352	362.86	33352	258.43	33352	218.14
33353	363.17	358.57	33353	359.19	33353	255.26	33353	217.72
33354	360.22	356.56	33354	358.91	33354	255.12	33354	217.74
33357	360.92	353.49	33357	353.49	33357	253.47	33357	216.15
33358	357.84	353.18	33358	355.42	33358	254.9	33358	216.18
33359	360.9	355.26	33359	360.85	33359	257.82	33359	216.54
33360	362.54	359.63	33360	360.6	33360	256.81	33360	216.12
33361	361.28	358.54	33361	360.54	33361	256.45	33361	215.55
33364	360.54	357.57	33364	359.93	33364	255.98	33364	216.45
33365	360.6	356.6	33365	356.63	33365	255.3	33365	215.82
33366	358.99	355.46	33366	358.07	33366	256.38	33366	215.12
33367	364.22	358.07	33367	363.77	33367	259.22	33367	215.22
33368	364.65	355.51	33368	355.78	33368	253.18	33368	214.06
33371	357.78	354.91	33371	357.54	33371	251.53	33371	214.22
33372	357.54	351.97	33372	353.15	33372	247.14	33372	214.32

Figure 9–3 Shows the Lotus 1, 2, 3 spreadsheet after all the files are combined using the command *File Combine*.

The poor performance of the Dow, OEX, and volume are not surprising. The Dow and the OEX are colinear to each other, and colinear to the S&P 500. Therefore they confuse the network. Colinear inputs are those which have essentially the same information in a slightly different form. The S&P 500 and the Dow 30 are examples of colinear inputs. They are almost the same, but not quite. The network gets confused; because of the slight differences, it does not know which one of the two to use and may alternate back and forth.

DATE	OEX-HIGH	OEX-LOW	OIL	UTILITY	CRB	GOLD	VOLUME
33340	360.13	355.73	253.86	218.18	220.71	84.81	229420
33343	361.67	358.01	256.49	218.81	220.58	83.43	218910
33344	366.75	358.96	258.68	220.89	220.57	83.06	257900
33345	370.1	366.04	259.86	219.76	220.16	83.99	327500
33346	370.01	367.09	258.39	216.3	218.04	81.64	252520
33347	367.86	363.67	256.63	212.65	217.72	80.82	237760
33350	365.1	360.49	254.98	210.95	217.79	83.35	211280
33351	363.89	359.5	257.71	209.51	217.95	82.87	185520
33352	363.18	359.96	258.43	210.39	218.14	82.17	202080
33353	363.17	358.57	255.26	209.38	217.72	79.8	174770
33354	360.22	356.56	255.12	209.82	217.74	79.74	173310
33357	360.92	353.49	253.47	208.31	216.15	78.17	163820
33358	357.84	353.18	254.9	210.01	216.18	80.57	266030
33359	360.9	355.26	257.82	212.09	216.54	79.84	215330
33360	362.54	359.63	256.81	211.9	216.12	80.59	182340
33361	361.28	358.54	256.45	211.46	215.55	78.83	171260
33364	360.54	357.57	255.98	211.96	216.45	80.1	151990
33365	360.6	356.6	255.3	211.52	215.82	80.33	166270
33366	358.99	355.46	256.38	213.41	215.12	79.82	183160
33367	364.22	358.07	259.22	214.1	215.22	80.01	214250
33368	364.65	355.51	253.18	210.39	214.06	77.97	235450

Figure 9–4 Shows the first 22 lines of the spreadsheet after all the date columns (except 1) have been deleted. The total spreadsheet has more than 800 rows of which only 22 are shown here.

GOLD		OEX			DOW-VOL		UTILI		TRANSP	
33343	83.43	33343	361.67	358.01	33343	218910	33343	218.81	33344	1143.1
33344	83.06	33344	366.75	358.96	33344	257900	33344	220.89	33345	1166.05
33345	83.99	33345	370.1	366.04	33345	327500	33345	219.76	33346	1178.01
33346	81.64	33346	370.01	367.09	33346	252520	33346	216.3	33347	1172.01
33347	80.82	33347	367.86	363.67	33347	237760	33347	212.65	33350	1151.12
33350	83.35	33350	365.1	360.49	33350	211280	33350	210.95	33351	1157.02
33351	82.87	33351	363.89	359.5	33351	185520	33351	209.51	33352	1171
33352	82.17	33352	363.18	359.96	33352	202080	33352	210.39	33353	1170.03
33353	79.8	33353	363.17	358.57	33353	174770	33353	209.38	33354	1166.02
33354	79.74	33354	360.22	356.56	33354	173310	33354	209.82	33357	1148.16
33357	78.17	33357	360.92	353.49	33357	163820	33357	208.31	33358	1142.16
33358	80.57	33358	357.84	353.18	33358	266030	33358	210.01	33359	1164.03
33359	79.84	33359	360.9	355.26	33359	215330	33359	212.09	33360	1168.07
33360	80.59	33360	362.54	359.63	33360	182340	33360	211.9	33361	1171.14
33361	78.83	33361	361.28	358.54	33361	171260	33361	211.46	33364	1177.11
33364	80.1	33364	360.54	357.57	33364	151990	33364	211.96	33365	1175.01
33365	80.33	33365	360.6	356.6	33365	166270	33365	211.52	33366	1178.05
33366	79.82	33366	358.99	355.46	33366	183160	33366	213.41	33367	1202.11
33367	80.01	33367	364.22	358.07	33367	214250	33367	214.1	33368	1187.05
33368	77.97	33368	364.65	355.51	33368	235450	33368	210.39	33371	1181.01
33371	79.45	33371	357.78	354.91	33371	178190	33371	211.02	33372	1159.14
33372	79.52	33372	357.54	351.97	33372	192530	33372	208.82	33373	1140.17

Figure 9–3 (Continued)

Normally, raw volume data is not used with neural networks because it is very noisy and volatile. One or more moving averages of volume are often used as an input.

The low of the S&P 500 is another input making a small contribution to the solution. At a future time, we may want to use it to reference the lower limit of a Bollinger Band; therefore, we are going to keep it in the input mix for the time being.

TRANSP	MA-VOL	TRANS_10	LEAD5	OEX-CL
1128.17	220503	1109.1	365.1	359.73
1123.05	218718	1101.11	361.51	360.48
1143.1	220164	1115.09	361.35	366.75
1166.05	221625	1116.04	362.86	368.67
1178.01	219618	1121.13	359.19	367.85
1172.01	220447	1114.19	358.91	365.1
1151.12	219380	1123.05	353.49	361.51
1157.02	220055	1111.12	355.42	361.35
1171	220691	1113.17	360.85	362.86
1170.03	220177	1121.02	360.6	359.19
1166.02	217619	1128.17	360.54	358.91
1148.16	210286	1123.05	359.93	353.49
1142.16	213474	1143.1	356.63	355.42
1164.03	212222	1166.05	358.07	360.85
1168.07	209727	1178.01	363.77	360.6
1171.14	207528	1172.01	355.78	360.54
1177.11	206783	1151.12	357.54	359.93
1175.01	206729	1157.02	353.15	356.63
1178.05	204290	1171	350.75	358.07
1202.11	203004	1170.03	354.13	363.77
1187.05	204886	1166.02	354.34	355.78

Figure 9–4 (Continued)

Table 9–1   Shows the relative contribution of each of the inputs when used to train a back-propagation network. Ranking is in reverse order. Inputs making the most contribution are at the bottom of the ranking.

Contribution	Input
1.22976	VOLUME
1.31203	OEX
1.76214	TRIN
1.97092	S&P500-L
2.21308	DOW-30
2.41897	UTIL
2.41966	TRANS
3.02431	GOLDSILV
3.20924	S&P500-C
3.57766	S&P500-H
3.69604	CRB
3.87979	OIL

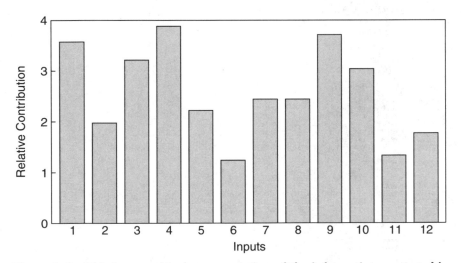

Figure 9–5   This is a graphical representation of the information presented in Table 9–1. The inputs are as follows: (1) S&P-high, (2) S&P-low, (3) S&P-close, (4) Oil, (5) Dow-30, (6) Dow-30 Volume, (7) Utility Index, (8) Transportation Index, (9) CRB, (10) Gold and Silver Mining Index, (11) OEX, and (12) TRIN.

DETERMINING A SUITABLE
MOVING AVERAGE FOR THE VOLUME INPUT

The next step will be to train the network again after deleting raw volume, the OEX, the TRIN, and the Dow 30. A 3-day, 5-day, and 10-day moving average of volume will be added, and the network trained again to find out which inputs contribute the most to the solution.

Table 9–2 and Figure 9–6 show the contributions of this set of inputs. Notice that the moving averages of volume now contribute more than the S&P 500 low. However, we do not know if we have the right period for volume because the largest period shows the greatest improvement as contributor to the solution. Because we never reached a peak performance, we do not know whether 10 days is the best period. It may be that a 20- or even a 100-day period is better.

Therefore, in an effort to end up with the best volume moving average, we are going to train the network again, using 10-, 20-, 30-, and 40-day moving averages of volume. Table 9–3 and Figure 9–7 show the results of this test run. Notice that the 30-day moving average of volume has become the fourth most important input, far ahead of 20- and 40-day moving averages. Because the 40-day period was less important than the 30-day average, we can assume that we have located the best choice. This run took 693,200 learning events to train and after training had an average mean error of 0.00178 when tested with the out-of-sample file, that is new, fresh, data.

Table 9–2   A ranking of the contribution of the inputs after raw volume, OEX, and Trin have been deleted and a 3-, 5-, and 10-day moving averages of volume have been added.

Contribution	Inputs
1.74687	S&P500-L
1.80293	MvAvg(5) of VOLUME
1.87156	MvAvg(3) of VOLUME
2.31732	MvAvg(10) of VOLUME
2.79877	S&P500-H
3.35121	S&P500-C
3.46610	TRANS
3.59537	GOLDSILV
3.95347	CRB
4.33959	UTIL
5.46879	OIL

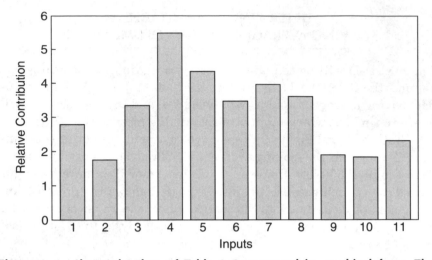

Figure 9–6 Shows the data of Table 9–2 presented in graphical form. The three moving averages of volume occupy the last three input positions (positions 9, 10, and 11).

Table 9–3 Here the three moving averages of volume of Figures 9–7 and 9–8 have been replaced with 10-, 20-, and 40-days moving average of volume.

Contributions	Inputs
1.86366	S&P500-L
2.18126	MvAvg(10) of VOLUME
2.74433	MvAvg(20) of VOLUME
2.83724	TRANS
2.96086	MvAvg(40) of VOLUME
3.11930	S&P500-H
3.15833	S&P500-C
3.31325	UTIL
3.58407	MvAvg(30) of VOLUME
3.61497	CRB
4.01614	GOLDSILV
5.45404	OIL

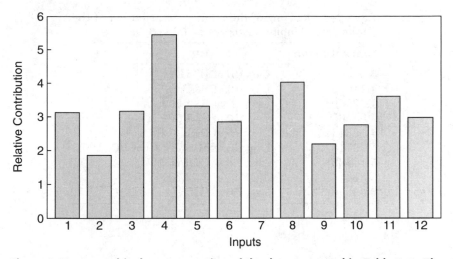

Figure 9–7 A graphical representation of the data presented in Table 9–3. The four moving averages occupy positions 9, 10, 11, and 12. Note the peak at position 11, which is the 30-day moving average of volume.

DETERMINING WHICH INPUTS
TO LAG AND NUMBER OF DAYS TO LAG

Lagging inputs, that is, inputs from 5, 10, or even 50 days in the past, often have great forecasting ability. Therefore, in an effort to see which inputs might have value as lagged inputs, we are going to train the network using just these lagged inputs:

    10-Day lag of S&P 500 High
    10-Day lag of S&P 500 Low
    10-Day lag of S&P 500 Close
    10-Day lag of Oil Index
    10-Day lag of Dow Utility Index
    10-Day lag of Dow Transportation Index
    10-Day lag of CRB Index
    10-Day lag of Gold and Silver Mining Index
    10-Day lag of 30-day Moving Average of Volume

The results of that training exercise are shown in Table 9–4 and Figure 9–8. Notice how input 4, Oil, makes the most contribution,

Table 9–4   Ranking of the relative contribution of the 10-day lagged inputs. Compare to Table 9–1.

Contribution	Inputs
3.95614	Lag(10) of UTIL
4.11610	Lag(10) of S&P500-C
4.33969	Lag(10) of S&P500-L
4.34565	Lag(10) of S&P500-H
4.58643	Lag(10) of CRB
4.79716	Lag(10) of MvAvg(30) of VOLUME
5.14433	Lag(10) of GOLDSILV
5.36414	Lag(10) of TRANS
7.45319	Lag(10) of OIL

about 60 or 70 percent better than the two next best inputs, Trans and Gold. To show the value of lagged inputs, this network took 880,600 events to train and has a mean average error of 0.00174 on the test data. This is slightly better than the 0.00178 of the previous network.

To determine the best lag for Oil, the network was trained with lags of 5, 10, 15, and 20-days. The inputs for the network were:

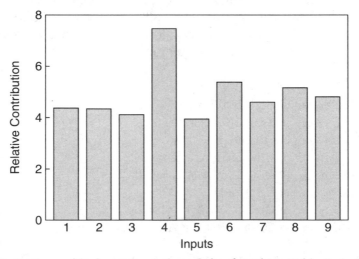

Figure 9–8   A graphical representation of the data from Table 9–4. See the text for a list of the inputs.

S&P 500 High
S&P 500 Low
S&P 500 Close
Oil Index
Dow Jones Transportation Index
CRB Index
Gold and Silver Mining Index
30-Day Moving Average of Volume
5-Day lag of Oil Index
10-Day lag of Oil Index
15-Day lag of Oil Index
20-Day lag of Oil Index

The 10-day lag of oil was the best of the four lags tested. It was the 3rd best input. Notice how the inputs ranking in Table 9–5 have been shuffled compared to Table 9–4, where Table 9–5 presents the results of training the network to determine the optimum lag of oil. Figure 9–9 presents the information in graphical form. Compare to Figure 9–7.

This latest network took 543,000 events to train and had a mean average test error of 0.00154. This was the smallest error recorded to date and more than 25 percent better than using just the basic 8 inputs by themselves.

Table 9–5   A ranking of the inputs when oil is lagged 10, 15, and 20 days.

Relative Contribution	Inputs
2.22390	S&P500-L
2.75324	Lag(5) of OIL
3.00056	CRB
3.17198	MvAvg(30) of VOLUME
3.42611	OIL
3.45828	Lag(20) of OIL
3.56932	S&P500-H
3.61248	TRANS
3.61321	Lag(15) of OIL
3.61448	S&P500-C
3.78064	Lag(10) of OIL
4.06948	UTIL
4.42846	GOLDSILV

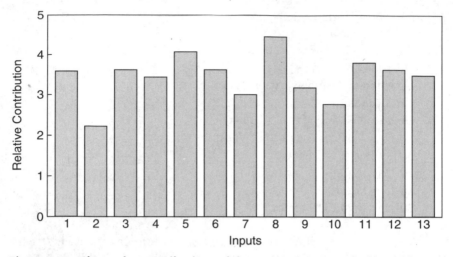

Figure 9–9 Shows the contributions of the various inputs ranked in Table 9–5. The first 10 inputs are the standard inputs and inputs 11 through 13 are the lagged oil inputs.

At this point, the reader should be able to see what we are trying to accomplish. First, we determined the optimum number of days over which to average the volume. Next, we determined that a 15-day lag of oil was optimum. Eventually, we will determine the optimum lags for the Gold and Silver Mining Index as well as the Transportation Index; then we will determine values of moving averages for the inputs making the most contribution. Finally, we will try several technical indicators to see if they can improve our results. By this time, we will have quite an array of inputs to choose from, both natural and processed. We will then weed them down to the optimum collection.

We are now going to lag the Gold and Silver Mining Index by 5, 10, 15, and 20 days to determine its optimum lag. As you can see by examining Table 9–6 and Figure 9–10, inputs 10, 11, 12, and 13 which correspond to the 5-, 10-, 15-, and 20-day lags, do not reach a clearly defined peak. That is to say, the contributions do not start small, go to a peak and then decline again. At this point, we do not know whether a 20-day or 100-day lag is the optimum one; therefore, we must run the exercise again, this time trying 10-, 20-, 30-, and 40-day lags.

Running into snags like this is normal in developing a neural network. Only by *trying* and *testing* can we find out what works and what does not. It is the time spent testing and exploring that separates so-so networks from those that give reliable forecasts time after time. We are seeking multiple diverse inputs that have a high predictive rela-

Table 9–6   Similar to Table 9–5 except in this case the
Gold and Silver Mining Index has been lagged 5-, 10-,
15-, 20-day periods.

Inputs	Relative Contributions
1.62168	Lag(5) of GOLDSILV
1.86548	Lag(15) of GOLDSILV
2.15252	Lag(10) of GOLDSILV
3.44518	S&P500-L
3.63554	Lag(20) of GOLDSILV
3.74607	TRANS
3.83964	S&P500-C
3.85705	GOLDSILV
3.93033	S&P500-H
4.46468	MvAvg(30) of VOLUME
4.53664	UTIL
5.38466	OIL
5.40981	CRB

tionship to the output, and only by applying imagination to the preprocessing and then testing those ideas can we approach the optimum
network. As with other ideals, the optimum network can never be obtained, only approached. The more you work, the closer you get.

Table 9–7 and Figure 9–11 show the results of this training process. Compare Figure 9–11 to Figure 9–10. Notice inputs 10, 11, 12,

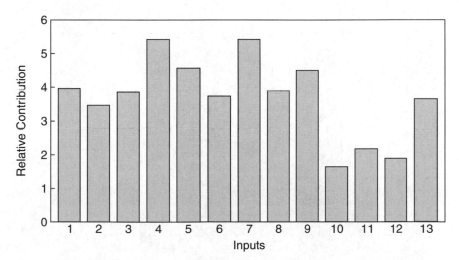

Figure 9–10   Gold and Silver Mining Index lagged 5, 10, 15, and 20 days. No
peak has been established.

Table 9–7 Here we are using Gold and Silver Mining
Index data lagged 10, 20, 30, and 40 days. Notice that
none of the Gold and Silver Mining Index lags made a
large contribution to the solution. This is attributed to
these 4 inputs being colinear.

1.51651	Lag(10) of GOLDSILV
2.38571	Lag(30) of GOLDSILV
2.51152	Lag(40) of GOLDSILV
2.54426	Lag(20) of GOLDSILV
2.73408	S&P500-L
2.77273	TRANS
3.46385	S&P500-H
3.55830	GOLDSILV
3.60025	S&P500-C
3.73590	MvAvg(30) of VOLUME
4.07699	UTIL
4.16612	CRB
5.09664	OIL

and 13 look smashed down in Figure 9–11 compared to 9–10. What
this is telling us is that the inputs in Figure 9–10, the last training
run, are probably colinear, and in all likelihood we are not getting a
true picture of which inputs are really making the best contribution.

One solution to this problem would be to test the network four
times, where each test uses only one of the four inputs, then compare
the mean average error of the four tests. Unfortunately, with a back-

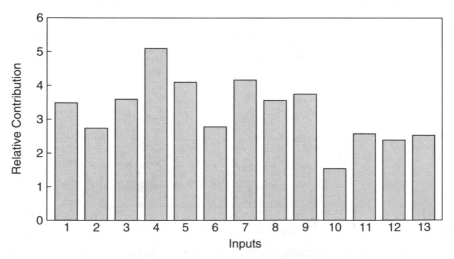

Figure 9–11 This is a graphical presentation of Table 9–7.

Table 9–8 Shows the results of training the network with just one of the lagged inputs at any given time. It also shows that the best input is a Gold and Silver Index lagged 40 days.

Gold and Silver Index	
Number of Days of Lag	**Mean Average Error**
0	0.000553
10	0.000522
20	0.000504
30	0.000507
40	0.000455
50	0.000494

propagation network, using a 486DX-33 computer, it takes 2 to 3 hours to train a network. Therefore we are talking about 8 to 12 hours of training time. However, a GRNN network trains in three minutes, but does not give either numeric or graphical data on relative contributions. The GRNN network gives the mean average test error; the lower the error the more accurate the network. In order to determine the best lag of the Gold and Silver Index, GSI, the GRNN network was trained first with no lagged GSI, then with lagged GSIs of 10-, 20-, 30-, 40-, and (surprise, because a minimum error had not been reached) 50-day lags.

Table 9–8 and Figure 9–12 show that the optimum lag of the Gold and Silver Index is 40 days.

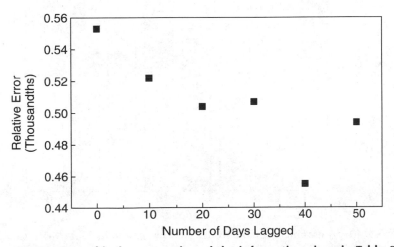

Figure 9–12 A graphical presentation of the information given in Table 9–9. The dip in the graph at 40 is typical of neural network experimentation.

DETERMINING WHICH MOVING
AVERAGE PERIOD MAKES THE LARGEST CONTRIBUTION

To find which moving average period, applied to the inputs has the greater effect, we will train a network using the 10-day moving average of all the inputs except volume, then a 20-day moving average of the inputs, and so on. Keep in mind that the inputs to the network will only be the moving average of original inputs; the original inputs will not be included.

Table 9–9 and Figure 9–13 show the results of training the network using the 10-day moving average of each of the inputs. The 10-day moving average of Utilities, Oil, CRB, and Transportation Indexes

Table 9–9   Here we are testing the data using a 10-day moving average of the data across all inputs.

2.09745	MvAvg(10) of S&P500-L
2.48538	MvAvg(10) of GOLDSILV
2.77351	MvAvg(10) of S&P500-C
3.14686	MvAvg(10) of S&P500-H
3.34438	MvAvg(10) of TRANS
3.37550	MvAvg(10) of CRB
3.95879	MvAvg(10) of OIL
4.15924	MvAvg(10) of UTIL

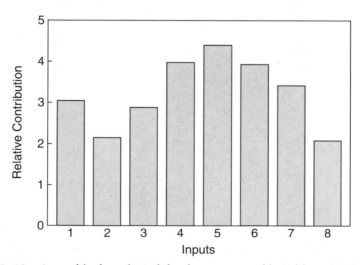

Figure 9–13   A graphical version of the data presented in Table 9–10. Compare to Figure 9–12.

seems to make a major contribution to the solution of the network. Next we try using a 20-day moving average of the inputs.

Table 9–10 and Figure 9–14 show the contributions of the 20-day moving average of the inputs. These results are almost a carbon copy of the results shown in Table 9–9 and Figure 9–13. The only real change is the increase in the contribution of the Transports. This is important when it becomes time to pick inputs; the 20-day moving average of Transportation is a better input than the 10-day moving average of Transportation.

Table 9–10   This is similar to Figure 9–21 except that a 20-day average is used instead of a 10-day moving average.

Contribution	Inputs
2.05892	MvAvg(20) of GOLDSILV
2.13794	MvAvg(20) of S&P500-L
2.86380	MvAvg(20) of S&P500-C
3.03801	MvAvg(20) of S&P500-H
3.37122	MvAvg(20) of CRB
3.89471	MvAvg(20) of TRANS
3.93819	MvAvg(20) of OIL
4.36914	MvAvg(20) of UTIL

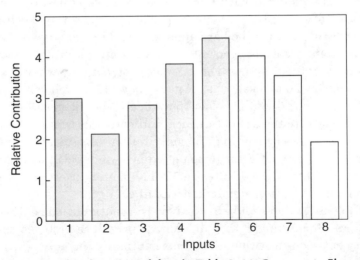

Figure 9–14   Graphical version of data in Table 9–11. Compare to Figures 9–12 and 9–13.

Table 9–11   Here a 30-day moving average was used.

Contribution	Inputs
1.89894	MvAvg(30) of GOLDSILV
2.12143	MvAvg(30) of S&P500-L
2.80172	MvAvg(30) of S&P500-C
2.98514	MvAvg(30) of S&P500-H
3.51706	MvAvg(30) of CRB
3.81150	MvAvg(30) of OIL
3.99805	MvAvg(30) of TRANS
4.43341	MvAvg(30) of UTIL

The results of the test using 30-day moving averages are shown in Table 9–11 and Figure 9–14. These results are almost the same as those obtained using a 20-day moving average, and very similar to the results from the 10-day moving average. It would appear that when an input had a contribution to make as moving average, the length of the moving average was inconsequential.

TECHNICAL INDICATORS

The number of technical indicators that could be applied to the network is almost limitless. Appendix B lists approximately 170 indicators that are included with one neural network software program. Almost all of the indicators can be varied in some way, such as the time period over which they are applied. In addition, buy and sell signals may come from the penetration of any limit at any precision that is assigned by the designer. For example, you can buy when the 7-day RSI goes below 20 and sell when it goes above 80, or you can buy when the 14-day stochastic falls below 15 and sell when it moves above 85.

To illustrate the use of technical indicators as inputs to a neural network, we will try finding the contribution of several common indicators. The first indicator to be tested is a 12-day RSI as defined by Wilder. In addition, we will test a 12-day moving average of this 12-day RSI that can often signal directional changes.

Table 9–12 and Figure 9–15 show the contributions of these two indicators. Surprisingly, they did very poorly. It is probable that colinearity between the two indicators is confusing the network. We will test the indicators individually. The first test of the 12-day RSI is presented in Table 9–13 and Figure 9–16.

Table 9–12   The basic inputs with a 12-day RSI and a 12-day moving average of the 12-day RSI.

Contribution	Inputs
1.40279	CRB
1.73755	TRANS
1.81674	WilderRSI(12) of S&P500-C
1.86036	MvAvg(12) of WilderRSI(12) of S&P500-C
1.97205	UTIL
2.21270	GOLDSILV
2.50631	OIL
2.91393	S&P500-L
3.38531	S&P500-C
3.98386	S&P500-H

The RSI fared much better, fourth out of nine indicators, and seems to help the other indicators to make significant contributions. This can be seen by comparing Figure 9–16 to Figure 9–15. Also, the original network with both indicators reached a mean average test error of 0.00218 while the network using only the RSI reached a mean average test error of 0.00190.

The test using the 12-day moving average of the 12-day RSI are presented in Table 9–14 and Figure 9–17. The results are much better than the network which used both the RSI and a moving average

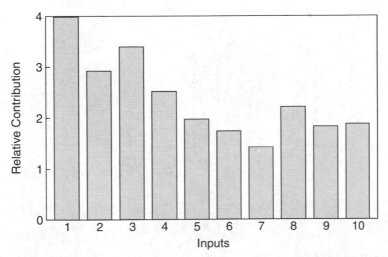

Figure 9–15   A graph of the data presented in Table 9–12. Input 9 is the 12-day RSI and Input 10 the 12-day moving average of the 12-day RSI.

Table 9–13   Here we have added just the 12-day RSI to the basic inputs. Notice that it is the fourth strongest input.

Contribution	Inputs
2.35697	S&P500-L
2.55498	TRANS
2.84366	UTIL
2.92278	CRB
2.94794	GOLDSILV
2.95302	WilderRSI(12) of S&P500-C
3.14279	OIL
3.56224	S&P500-C
3.60003	S&P500-H

of the RSI, but not as good as the network which used just the RSI by itself. As expected, the mean average test error fell between the values for the other networks at 0.00206. The network using the 12-day RSI by itself is the best choice. This determination could have been carried on further by trying different periods for the RSI, then trying different moving averages of each of the RSI periods.

Next we are going to see whether Bollinger Bands make good inputs. Bollinger Bands are lines drawn above and below the price data.

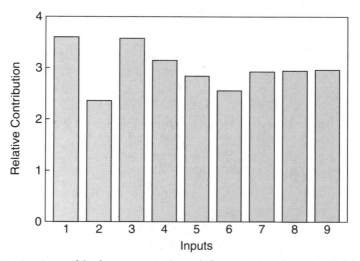

Figure 9–16   A graphical representation of the material shown in Table 9–13. The RSI is the ninth input.

Table 9–14   The 12-period moving average of the 12-day RSI have been added to the basic inputs. It is not as good a contributor as the RSI by itself.

2.09485	S&P500-L
2.12979	MvAvg(12) of WilderRSI(12) of S&P500-C
2.37479	TRANS
2.92374	S&P500-C
3.14522	GOLDSILV
3.18821	CRB
3.25310	OIL
3.52732	UTIL
3.76387	S&P500-H

The bands are usually set at 2 standard deviations of a 20-period moving average above and below the price data. Figure 9–18 shows the S&P 500, with Bollinger Bands on both sides of the daily price data. Penetration of the bands by the price data usually, but not always, leads to a reversal in trend.

Table 9–15 and Figure 9–19 show the results of training the network using the data for the low and high Bollinger Bands. These bands were placed 2 standard deviations from a 20-day moving average of the S&P 500. Notice that the bands made more of a contribution to

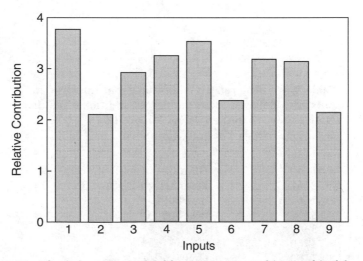

Figure 9–17   The information of Table 9–14 presented in graphical form. The ninth input is the 12-period moving average of the 12-day RSI.

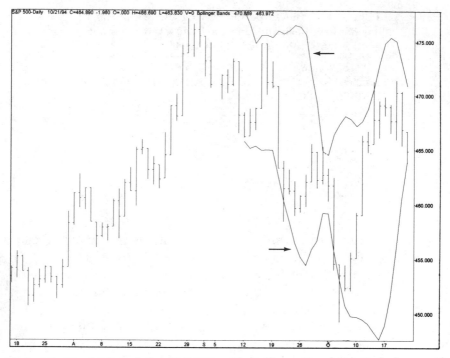

S&P 500-Daily 10/21/94 C=484.890 -1.980 O=.000 H=486.890 L=483.830 V=0 Bollinger Bands 470.889 463.972

Figure 9–18 A plot of the S&P-500 with Bollinger Bands plotted above and below the price data. Arrows point to the bands.

Table 9–15 The relative contribution of the basic inputs with Bollinger Bands added as additional inputs. Notice they fell in the 7th and 8th positions.

1.84469	S&P500-L
2.41241	TRANS
2.51149	BBandLow(20,2) of S&P500-C
2.56552	BBandHigh(20,2) of S&P500-C
2.57661	S&P500-C
2.76961	S&P500-H
3.33409	UTIL
3.74759	OIL
3.87163	GOLDSILV
4.08155	CRB

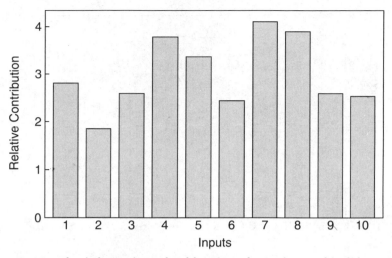

Figure 9–19 The information of Table 9–15 shown in graphical form. The Bollinger Bands are inputs 9 and 10.

the solution of the problem than either the Dow Transports or the low of the S&P 500.

Next, we'll try a 12-day momentum indicator which the computer calls "change(12) of S&P500-C." This indicator measures the change in price over the last 12 days, that is, today's price less the price of 12 days ago. Table 9–16 and Figure 9–20 show the results of that test. Notice that the momentum function makes a fairly large contribution, and is fourth on the list, and being ahead of Gold/Silver Mining Index, CRB, and Transports among others. It is 1 full point better than the Bollinger Band contribution.

Table 9–16 Here we have added Momentum Indicator (Change(12) of S&P-500-C). Here it is the fourth strongest input.

2.22728	S&P500-L
2.82420	TRANS
3.11503	CRB
3.20623	S&P500-C
3.32080	GOLDSILV
3.50186	Change(12) of S&P500-C
3.53974	OIL
3.55968	UTIL
3.59859	S&P500-H

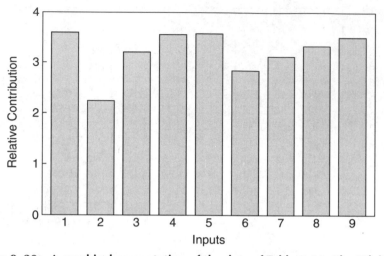

Figure 9–20 A graphical presentation of the data of Table 9–16. The 9th input is the momentum indicator.

SELECTING THE DEFINITIVE INPUTS

Testing has created a large number of possible indicators from moving averages and lagged inputs to technical indicators. The problem now is to select the few that will best help the solution of the problem. The basic inputs will be the following:

S&P 500 High
S&P 500 Low
S&P 500 Close
Oil Index
Dow Utilities Index
CRB Index
Gold and Silver Mining Index

To these inputs we will add the four inputs which scored the highest when tested with the original 7 inputs:

Added Input	Contribution
Lag(10) of CRB	5.11
Lag(10) of Gold and Silver Mining Index	5.14
Lag(10) of Dow Transportation Index	5.36
Lag(10) of Oil	7.45

We will add a 30-period moving average of volume. Note that no moving averages other than volume are included, and that no indicators are included. The lags chosen all had contributions above 5.00 and were the only inputs which had scores above 5.00. The technical indicators had contributions in the range of 2.50 and 3.50. Moving averages had scores in the range of 3.00 and 4.50.

These inputs were tested as a group using the back-propagation network. The results of this test are shown in Table 9–17 and Figure 9–21. Note that input 11, lag(10) of the Gold and Silver Mining Index is substantially below the rest of the inputs. Therefore, for final training, this input will be dropped, because we want to use only the most robust inputs.

THE FINAL NETWORK

Previous work has shown that networks based on financial series work best when the network architecture is a General Regression Neural Network (GRNN). Therefore, the final inputs for our model were trained using a GRNN network. There were 96 out-of-sample test patterns. Figure 9–22 shows a graph of the mean squared error versus smoothing factor for this network. During training, the network assumes a smoothing factor, then tests it; it then tries another smoothing

Table 9–17 Shows the contributions the almost finished network. Here the number of inputs numbers 13. As described in the text the Lag of the Gold and Silver Mining Index will be dropped from the final network.

1.96568	Lag(10) of GOLDSILV
2.65485	S&P500-C
2.68148	S&P500-H
2.84308	S&P500-L
3.07333	TRANS
3.33825	MvAvg(30) of VOLUME
3.34365	CRB
3.65791	Lag(10) of CRB
3.73944	GOLDSILV
3.82980	UTIL
4.70225	OIL
4.72849	Lag(10) of OIL
4.75725	Lag(10) of TRANS

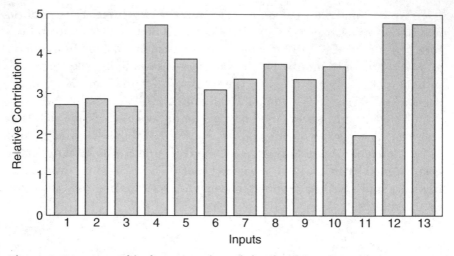

Figure 9–21 A graphical presentation of the data given in Table 9–17. Input 11 is the Gold and Silver Mining Index.

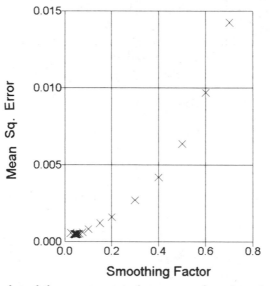

Figure 9–22 A plot of the mean squared error as a function of the smoothing factor.

factor and tests it. This process continues until the network finds the smoothing factor with the lowest mean squared error.

The GRNN network had a smoothing factor of 0.04551 and the mean squared error was 0.000505. The mean average error was 1.965. The same inputs with a 3-layer back-propagation network having 12 hidden neurons yielded a mean average error of 4.038. The GRNN network with the same inputs is more than twice as accurate as the back-propagation network. This is particularly interesting because it was the same back-propagation network which was used to grade and select the inputs.

GENETIC ALGORITHM—GRNN NETWORK

Ward Systems Group recently released their *Neural Shell 2,*® version 2.0. This release contains a new genetic algorithm (GA) based network paradigm. When used with PNN and GRNN networks, it finds an individual smoothing factor for each input as well as a smoothing factor for the overall network. It was said to be twice as accurate when used with time-series networks. It also included a sensitivity function which measured the contribution of each input, something which has been missing from the previous PNN and GRNN networks. The tradeoff for this increased accuracy was longer training time, several hours compared with 2 or 3 minutes.

The inputs used for the final GRNN network were used with the new GA-GRNN network. The mean-squared error was 0.0004181 and the mean error was 1.843. This was about a 20 percent improvement; better, but not the doubling hoped for. However, the sensitivity function indicated that the S&P 500 close, the Dow 30 and the TRIN could be deleted. When this was done, the mean-squared error dropped to 0.000235, and this time the sensitivity function indicated that removal of the OEX function would improve the results. The OEX function was removed and the network trained again. However, the sensitivity function indicated that removal of the Dow Transportation input would improve things further. Again this was done and the network retrained. However, the network was now calling for the removal of the lag of the Gold and Silver Mining Index.

This training resulted in a network which was happy with the remaining inputs and had a mean-squared error of 0.0002992 and a mean error of 1.53. The mean squared error of 0.0002992 is nearly one-half of the 0.0004551 of the GRNN network, and the mean error of 1.53 is better than the 1.843 recorded by the GRNN network. Figure 9–23 gives the error data when tested with fresh data.

To put this data in a different light, 38 percent of the data points were within one S&P 500 point of forecasting the value of the S&P 500 *10* days in advance. Seventy-six percent of the data forecasts were within two S&P points, and 93 percent of the forecasts were within four points.

Next, these pruned inputs were used with a GA-GRNN network to forecast the S&P 500 *five* days in advance with very impressive results. The mean squared error was 0.000217 and the average error was 1.268 S&P points. Fifty-six percent of the data points were within one point of the actual S&P 500 value. Seventy-seven percent of the points were within two S&P points and 99 percent were within four points. The error data can be examined in Figure 9–24.

TRADING WITH A NEURAL NETWORK

Neural network architecture and training algorithms are advancing at a remarkably fast pace. Sometime in the future, they will be the basis of a stand-alone trading system. However, at this time, it is best if they are used as a confirming indicator with one or more other indicators.

One system for trading the S&P 500 or the OEX might use Bollinger Bands as the primary indicator, and a 5-day stochastic or a 7-day RSI as a confirming indicator, and use the 5-day and 10-day neural forecasts to confirm the first two. For example, wait until the S&P 500 price moves above the upper band of the 20-day 2-standard deviation Bollinger Band. This usually means the upward trend is about to become a downward trend and lets you prepare for a sell signal. Wait until the overbought condition is confirmed by either the stochastic or the RSI indicator (your choice). Look at the forecasts of both the 5- and 10-day neural networks. If they anticipate a drop in value of, for example, 7 points in the next five days and 12 points in the next 10 days, it would be an excellent time to sell the market. However, if the neural network forecasts that the market would be up 7 and 12 points, then it would be a good time to sit on the sidelines until the neural network forecasts and the technical indicators confirm one another.

When trading options, one requirement for choosing a suitable option strategy is to know, approximately, the underlying security value

	A	B	C
1	Actual(1)	Network(1)	Act-Net(1)
2			
3			
4			
5	360.529998779297	353.294708251953	7.235290527344
6	360.309997558594	357.920196533203	2.389801025391
7	366.500000000000	366.160888671875	0.339111328125
8	367.010009765625	369.484771728516	-2.474761962891
9	356.910003662109	360.088043212891	-3.178039550781
10	370.399993896484	368.547821044922	1.852172851563
11	364.989990234375	365.711242675781	-0.721252441406
12	364.940002441406	363.374633789063	1.565368652344
13	366.809997558594	367.782897949219	-0.972900390625
14	367.760009765625	367.006958007813	0.753051757813
15	370.290008544922	368.756195068359	1.533813476563
16	353.820007324219	352.563262939453	1.256744384766
17	353.190002441406	356.158172607422	-2.968170166016
18	376.850006103516	372.762023925781	4.087982177734
19	385.750000000000	386.841888427734	-1.091888427734
20	386.730010986328	386.431457519531	0.298553466797
21	382.459991455078	384.964874267578	-2.504882812500
22	385.149993896484	384.944305419922	0.205688476563
23	378.790008544922	378.052581787109	0.737426757813
24	383.239990234375	382.199035644531	1.040954589844
25	381.269989013672	375.641418457031	5.628570556641
26	385.769989013672	386.662506103516	-0.892517089844
27	391.609985351563	391.492584228516	0.117401123047
28	392.809997558594	390.733764648438	2.076232910156
29	390.059997558594	389.030151367188	1.029846191406
30	381.500000000000	381.180969238281	0.319030761719
31	387.359985351563	385.000854492188	2.359130859375
32	390.160003662109	389.026611328125	1.133392333984
33	395.899993896484	393.755859375000	2.144134521484
34	390.230010986328	391.077148437500	-0.847137451172
35	384.029998779297	385.232543945313	-1.202545166016
36	388.630004882813	389.655578613281	-1.025573730469
37	382.049987792969	386.282958984375	-4.232971191406
38	368.570007324219	373.397491455078	-4.827484130859

Figure 9–23   Shows the error in S&P 500 points of the network when tested with out-of-sample data. The first column is the actual value and the second column is the forecast value and the third column is the error between the first two columns. Note that this forecast was for 10-days in the future.

	A	B	C
	Actual(1)	Network(1)	Act-Net(1)
1			
2			
3			
4			
5	364.279998779297	362.152130126953	2.127868652344
6	353.109985351563	356.289672851563	-3.179687500000
7	364.279998779297	363.466827392578	0.813171386719
8	366.390014648438	366.526123046875	-0.136108398438
9	368.279998779297	369.120361328125	-0.840362548828
10	372.359985351563	371.735626220703	0.624359130859
11	363.450012207031	364.362365722656	-0.912353515625
12	365.660003662109	364.732727050781	0.927276611328
13	357.730010986328	356.172149658203	1.557861328125
14	363.970001220703	363.599639892578	0.370361328125
15	363.799987792969	366.048217773438	-2.248229980469
16	355.559997558594	358.859527587891	-3.299530029297
17	354.839996337891	355.485748291016	-0.645751953125
18	358.869995117188	358.247985839844	0.622009277344
19	388.880004882813	387.594970703125	1.285034179688
20	392.829986572266	389.974639892578	2.855346679688
21	380.209991455078	383.875762939453	-3.665771484375
22	384.269989013672	383.539123535156	0.730865478516
23	384.649993896484	383.187225341797	1.462768554688
24	380.390014648438	382.448181152344	-2.058166503906
25	378.040008544922	378.218780517578	-0.178771972656
26	380.649993896484	380.900146484375	-0.250152587891
27	383.540008544922	384.393402099609	-0.853393554688
28	391.019989013672	390.416442871094	0.603546142578
29	388.660003662109	390.437500000000	-1.777496337891
30	385.230010986328	386.936645507813	-1.706634521484
31	381.070007324219	380.756439208984	0.313568115234
32	387.070007324219	386.716979980469	0.353027343750
33	384.890014648438	384.777160644531	0.112854003906
34	392.160003662109	391.416137695313	0.743865966797
35	389.709991455078	387.924865722656	1.785125732422
36	387.390014648438	386.829376220703	0.560638427734
37	392.299987792969	388.498504638672	3.801483154297
38	376.700012207031	377.882629394531	-1.182617187500
39	377.359985351563	375.857482910156	1.502502441406

Figure 9–24   This data is like the data of 9–10 except the forecast is for only 5 days. Naturally this data is more accurate than that given in Figure 9–23 for a 10 day forecast.

at some future time. There are many excellent programs for determining the correct strategy; however, they are only as good as the time and value predictions made by the individual using the program. A neural network forecast should be better than other methods of estimating the value of the underlying security 5 or 10 days into the future.

It is important that a near-term and a long-term forecast be used, because the near-term forecast is more accurate and is used to confirm the far-term forecast. If the long-term forecast anticipates 10 points rise by a certain date, and the near-term forecast for the same date says the market is going 10 points lower, it is best to believe the near-term forecast, or to step aside completely until the situation is resolved.

If the 10-day and 5-day neural network forecasts are both up and the technical indicators are also signaling an upward move, go for it.

Appendix A

A CASE STUDY

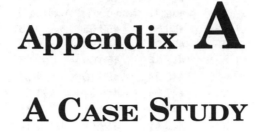

Throughout the book, a network called the *benchmark network* has been used to illustrate different points. This network was chosen because it trained relatively fast, used a back-propagation network and momentum training algorithm which are the most popular and well known. Further, the results were fairly good.

Using the lessons taught earlier in the book and using the same data, a new network was created which far surpasses the original benchmark net work. The network was expanded to 12 inputs by adding the 20-period moving average of each of the original six inputs. Next, rather than using the ever-popular back-propagation network, the 12 inputs were trained in a General Regression Neural Network (GRNN).

The forecast output and its error are presented in Figures A–1 and A–2. The statistics are given in Tables A–1 and A–2. The new network is nearly an order of magnitude better than the original network.

	A	B	C
1	Actual(1)	Network(1)	Act-Net(1)
2	450.50	450.05	0.45
3	450.08	449.90	0.18
4	448.64	450.69	-2.05
5	448.23	450.10	-1.87
6	448.04	449.97	-1.93
7	447.94	450.05	-2.11
8	448.41	449.58	-1.17
9	448.66	448.74	-0.08
10	449.22	448.59	0.63
11	448.38	448.37	0.01
12	447.29	448.26	-0.97
13	447.57	448.72	-1.15
14	447.55	448.93	-1.38
15	446.92	449.28	-2.36
16	446.55	447.90	-1.35
17	445.75	447.08	-1.33
18	446.30	447.45	-1.15
19	445.31	447.31	-2.00
20	445.34	446.88	-1.54
21	445.18	446.73	-1.55
22	445.70	446.21	-0.51
23	445.85	447.06	-1.21
24	446.02	446.53	-0.51
25	444.22	446.74	-2.52
26	445.79	446.58	-0.79
27	446.75	446.96	-0.21
28	447.49	447.01	0.48
29	447.08	447.17	-0.09
30	447.08	446.15	0.93
31	447.31	447.13	0.18
32	446.14	447.86	-1.72
33	446.48	448.25	-1.77
34	446.26	447.94	-1.68
35	446.46	447.95	-1.49
36	446.23	448.16	-1.93
37	446.39	446.76	-0.37
38	447.18	447.12	0.06

Figure A–1 Output and error of original benchmark network. Column A gives the actual data before training. Column B gives the network's forecast, and column C is the error or the difference between columns A and B. Mean squared error = 2.447, mean error = 1.265%, and time to train = 0:05:42.

	A	B	C
1	Actual(1)	Network(1)	Act-Net(1)
2			
3			
4			
5			

〰〰〰〰〰〰〰〰〰〰〰〰〰〰

	A	B	C
20			
21	445.18	445.70	-0.52
22	445.70	445.70	0.00
23	445.85	445.85	0.00
24	446.02	445.99	0.03
25	444.22	444.29	-0.07
26	445.79	445.77	0.02
27	446.75	446.80	-0.05
28	447.49	447.34	0.15
29	447.08	447.19	-0.11
30	447.08	447.08	0.00
31	447.31	446.17	1.14
32	446.14	446.19	-0.05
33	446.48	446.39	0.09
34	446.26	446.35	-0.09
35	446.46	446.40	0.06
36	446.23	446.24	-0.01
37	446.39	446.40	-0.01
38	447.18	447.07	0.11
39	446.44	446.59	-0.15
40	447.00	446.94	0.06
41	446.76	446.65	0.11
42	446.52	446.37	0.15
43	446.20	446.20	-0.00
44	444.11	444.12	-0.01
45	444.51	444.53	-0.02
46	446.58	446.37	0.21
47	445.79	445.86	-0.07
48	445.26	445.48	-0.22

Figure A–2 Output and error of modified benchmark network. The inputs have been doubled by adding 20-period moving averages of each of the input, and the network has been trained on a General Regression Neural Network (GRNN). The mean error has been reduced from 1.265 percent to 0.092 percent and the mean squared error from 2.447 to 0.52, while the time to train has been reduced from over 5 minutes to 32 seconds. Mean squared error = 0.052, mean error = 0.092%, and time to train = 0:00:32.

Table A–1   Comparison of original and new network inputs.

	Original Benchmark Network	New 12-Input Network
Inputs	ADV, DEC, TICK, TRIN, SPY, YXY	ADV, DEC, TICK, TRIN, SPY, YXY, MA(20)-ADV, MA(20)-DEC, MA(20)-TICK, MA(20)-TRIN, MA(20)-SPY, MA(20)-YXY

Table A–2   Comparision of statistics of back-propagation architecture vs. GRNN architecture.

Network Training Algorithm	Back-Propagation Momentum (0.05, 0.5)	General Regression Neural Network
Training time	5:42	00:32
R-Squared	0.9262	0.9984
Mean squared error	2.447	0.052
Mean error	1.265	0.092

Appendix B

NEURAL SHELL—MARKET INDICATORS

Accumulation/Distribution

Accumulation1—Call Open Interest

Accumulation1—Call Volume

Accumulation1—Pull Open Interest

Accumulation1—Put Volume

Accumulation1—Put+Call Open Interest

Accumulation1—Put+Call Volume

Accumulation1—Volume

Accumulation2—Call Open Interest

Accumulation2—Call Volume

Accumulation2—Open Interest

Accumulation2—Put Open Interest

Accumulation2—Put Volume

Accumulation2—Put+Call Open Interest

Accumulation2—Put+Call Volume

Accumulation2—Volume

Bollinger Band—%B

Bollinger Band—Band Width Percent

Bollinger Band—High

Bollinger Band—Low

Change—Net Change (Momentum)

Change—Percent Change

Change—Rate Of Change (Velocity)

Change—Rate of Rate Of Change (Acceleration)

Commodity Channel Index (CC)

Daily Change—# Negative Changes

Daily Change—# Pos minus # Neg (Dot)

Daily Change—# Positive Changes

Daily Change—Average Change

Daily Change—Average Negative Change

Daily Change—Average Positive Change

Daily Change—Sum of Negative Changes

Daily Change—Sum Of Positive Changes

Lag

Lagged Mov Avg—Exponential

Lagged Mov Avg—Linearly Weighted

Lagged Mov Avg—Simple

Lead (used on outputs to predict future periods)

Life Force—Call Open Interest

Life Force—Call Volume

Life Force—Open Interest

Life Force—Put Open Interest

Life Force—Put Volume

Life Force—Put+Call Open Interest

Life Force—Put+Call Volume

Life Force—Volume

Linear Regression—Coef of Determination (R2)

Linear Regression—Coef of Regression (slope)

Linear Regression—Predicted Change

Linear Regression—Predicted Value

Mass Index

Mov Avg—Exponential

Mov Avg—Linearly Weighted

Mov Avg—Simple

Mov Avg Diff—Exponential

Mov Avg Diff—Exponential & Lagged Exp

Mov Avg Diff—Lin Wgt & Lagged Lin Wgt

Mov Avg Diff—Linearly Weighted

Mov Avg Diff—Simple

Mov Avg Diff—Simple & Lagged Simple

Mov Avg Diff of Mov Avg Diff—Exponential (MACD)

Mov Avg of Mov Avg Diff—Linearly Weighted

Mov Avg of Mov Avg Diff—Simple

Moving Avg—Call Open Interest Weighted

Moving Avg—Call Volume Weighted

Moving Avg—Open Interest Weighted

Moving Avg—Put Open Interest Weighted

Moving Avg—Put Volume Weighted

Moving Avg—Put+Call Open Interest Weighted

Moving Avg—Put +Call Volume Weighted

Moving Avg—Volume Weighted

Negative Call Open Interest Index

Negative Call Volume Index

Negative Open Interest Index

Negative Put Open Interest Index

Negative Put Volume Index

Negative Put+Call Open Interest Index

Negative Put+Call Volume Index

Negative Volume Index

On Balance Call Open Interest

On Balance Call Volume

On Balance Open Interest

On Balance Put Open Interest

On Balance Put Volume

On Balance Put+Call Open Interest

On Balance Put+Call Volume

On Balance Volume

Positive Call Open Interest Index

Positive Call Volume Index

Positive Open Interest Index

Positive Put Open Interest Index

Positive Put Volume Index

Positive Put+Call Open Interest Index

Positive Put+Call Volume Index

Positive Volume Index

Price Trend—Call Open Interest

Price Trend—Call Volume

Price Trend—Open Interest

Price Trend—Put Open Interest

Price Trend—Put Volume

Price Trend—Put+Call Open Interest

Price Trend—Put+Call Volume

Price Trend—Volume

Range—Highest minus Lowest Value

Range—Highest Value

Range—Lowest Value

Relative Strength Index(RSI)—Cutler's

Relative Strength Index(RSI)—Wilder's

Resistance Index—Call Open Interest

Resistance Index—Call Volume

Resistance Index—Open Interest

Resistance Index—Put Open Interest

Resistance Index—Put+Call Open Interest

Resistance Index—Put+Call Volume

Resistance Index—Volume

Resistance to Advances—Call Open Interest

Resistance to Advances—Call Volume

Resistance to Advances—Open Interest

Resistance to Advances—Put Open Interest

Resistance to Advances—Put Volume

Resistance to Advances—Put+Call Open Interest

Resistance to Advances—Put+Call Volume

Resistance to Advances—Volume

Resistance to Declines—Call Open Interest

Resistance to Declines—Call Volume

Resistance to Declines—Open Interest

Resistance to Declines—Put Open Interest

Resistance to Declines—Put Volume

Resistance to Declines—Put+Call Open Interest

Resistance to Declines—Put+Call Volume

Resistance to Declines—Volume

Standard Deviation

Stochastic %D

Stochastic %K

Slow Stochastic %D

True Strength Indicator (TSI)

Wilder's Average Directional Movement (ADX)

Wilder's Directional Movement (DX)

William's %R

William's Variable Accum/Dist—Call Open Interest

William's Variable Accum/Dist—Call Volume

William's Variable Accum/Dist—Open Interest

William's Variable Accum/Dist—Put Open Interest

William's Variable Accum/Dist—Put Volume

William's Variable Accum/Dist—Put+Call Open Interest

William's Variable Accum/Dist—Put+Call Volume

William's Variable Accum/Dist—Volume

Appendix C

SUPPLIERS OF NEURAL NETWORK SOFTWARE

AbTech Corporation
508 Dale Avenue
Charlottesville, VA 22903
804-977-0686

AND America Ltd
2140 Winston Park Drive #202
Oakville, ON L6H5V5
416-829-0788

Al Ware, Inc.
11000 Cedar Avenue
Cleveland, OH 44106
216-421-2380

Applied Cognetics
5648 Riverdale Avenue #95
Riverdale, NY 10471
212-969-8769

ARD Corporation
9151 Rumsey Road
Columbia, MD 21045
410-997-5600

California Scientific Software
10024 Netown Road
Nevada City, CA 95959
916-478-9040

Charles River Analytics
55 Wheeler Street
Cambridge, MA 02138
617-491-3474

Cheshire Engineering Corp.
650 Sierra Madre Villa, Suite 201
Pasadena, CA 91107
818-351-0209

Cogito Software, Inc.
P.O. Box 451
Pine River, MN 56474
800-450-2001

Design Sciences Corporation
8300 Boone Blvd.
Vienna, VA 22182
703-848-9247

Gray Matter Tech, Inc.
388 Market Street #500
San Francisco, CA 94111
415-296-3825

Guffy Software
45 Bearman Road East
Rochester, NY 14624
716-594-2836

Future Wave Software
1330 S. Gertruda Avenue
Redondo Beach, CA 90277
310-540-5373

HyperLogic Corporation
1855 East Valley #210
Escondido, CA 92027
619-746-2765

IBM Corporation
3605 Highway 52 North
Rochester, MN 55901
800-342-6672

Inductive Solutions
380 Rector Place #4A
New York, NY 10280
212-945-0630

Intelligent Machines, Inc.
1153 Bordeaux Drive
Sunnyvale, CA 94089
408-745-0881

Intel Neural Network Group
2200 Mission College Boulevard
Santa Clara, CA 95052
408-765-9235

Itanis International, Inc.
1737 Holly Lane
Pittsburgh, PA 15216
412-344-4553

Lever Software Systems
P.O. Box 7168
University Station
Syracuse, NY 13210
800-638-7256

Logical Design Consulting
2015 Olite Court
La Jolla, CA 92037
619-459-6236

Maristream, Inc.
2015 Franklin Street
N. Little Rock, AR 72114
501-758-7482

Mendelsohn Enterprises, Inc.
25941 Apple Blossom Lane
Wesley Chapel, FL 33544
813-973-0496

Neural Computer Sciences
Unit 3 Lulworth Bus. Ctr.
Nutwood Way
Totton, Southampton, UK
SO43WW
44-703-667775

Neural Systems
2827 West 43rd Avenue
Vancouver, BC V6N3H9
604-263-3667

Neural Technologies, Ltd.
7a Lavent Street
Peterfield, Hampshire, UK
GU323EL
44-730-260256

NeuralWare, Inc.
Penn Center West, Building IV
Pittsburgh, PA 15276
412-787-8222

Neurix
327 A Street, 6th Floor
Boston, MA 02210
617-577-1202

NeuroDimension, Inc.
720 S.W. 2nd Avenue, #458
Gainesville, FL 32601
904-377-5144

NeuroDynamX, Inc.
P.O. Box 323
Boulder, CO 80306
303-442-2536

NIBS, Inc.
62 Fowlie Road
Singapore 1542
65-344-2357

Onuk and Berkan Associates
665 Thwaites Place, #2V
Bronx, NY 10467
718-798-5609

Promised Land Technologies
195 Church Street, 8th Floor
New Haven, CT 06510
203-562-7335

Rapid Imaging, Inc.
P.O. Box 678214
Orlando, FL 32867
407-282-1609

Reduct Systems, Inc.
P.O. Box 3570
Regina, SK 34P3L7
306-586-9408

Scientific Consultant Services
20 Stage Coach Road
Selden, NY 11784
516-696-3333

Software Frontiers Systems
P.O. Box 402
Gilbert, AZ 85234
602-985-8550

Talon Development Corp.
P.O. Box 11069
Milwaukee, WI 53211
414-962-7246

Telebyte Technology, Inc.
270 Pulaski Road
Greenlawn, NY 11740
516-423-3232

Teranet IA
1615 Bowen Road
Nanaimo, BC V9S1G5
604-754-4223

The MathWorks, Inc.
24 Prime Park Way
Natick, MA 01760
508-653-1415

Vesta Services, Inc.
1001 Green Bay Road, #196
Winnetka, IL 60093
708-446-1655

Ward Systems Group
Executive Park West
5 Hillcrest Drive
Frederick, MD 21702
301-662-7950

GLOSSARY

Absolute Error: The absolute error is the absolute value of the difference between the value the network is predicting for an output and the actual value of that output.

Advancing Issues (ADV): Number of securities advancing in a given period of time.

Architecture: A description of the number of the layers in a neural network, each layer's transfer function, the number of neurons per layer, and the connections between layers.

Artificial Neural Network (ANN): A software program intended to mimic the human brain's ability to classify patterns or to make forecasts based on past experience.

Average Error: The average of the error factors of all patterns.

Back-Propagation: A neural network architecture that compares the forecast output to the actual output as feedback to correct the learning process.

Benchmark: An object or process against which other objects or processes are compared. In many cases, the benchmark is the finest that can be produced. Benchmark can be the ideal, a realistic goal, or an average result used for comparison.

Bollinger Bands: An envelope plotted at a standard deviation above and below a moving average. Usually the standard deviation is 2.0 and the moving average is 20 periods long.

Contribution Factor: A number given to each input variable that is a rough measure of the importance of that variable in predicting the network's output, relative to other input variables in the same network. The higher the number, the more the variable is contributing to the forecast or classification.

Correlation Coefficient-R: A statistical measure of the strength of the relationship between the actual and predicted outputs. The R coefficient can range from -1 to $+1$. The closer R is to $+1$, the stronger the positive linear relationship, and the closer R is to -1 the stronger the negative linear relationship. When R is near 0 there is no relationship.

Declining Issues (DEC): The number of securities declining in price during a given period of time.

Epoch: A complete pass through the network of the entire set of training patterns.

Event: The presentation of a single training pattern to the neural network.

Generalization: The attribute of a network where the output for new input vectors tend to be close to the output for similar input vectors in its training set.

General Regression Neural Networks (GRNN): A 3-layer network where there must be one hidden neuron for each training pattern. They work by measuring how far a given sample pattern is from patterns in the training set in N dimensional space, where N is number of inputs in the problem. They train exceedingly fast.

Global Minimum: The lowest value of a function over the entire range of its input parameters. Gradient descent methods adjust weights and biases in order to find the global minimum of error for a network.

Gradient Descent: The process of making changes to weights and biases, where the changes are proportional to the derivatives of network error with respect to those weights and biases. This is done to minimize network error.

Input: A variable that a network uses to make a classification or prediction. Scientists label it an independent variable.

Local Minimum: The minimum value of a function over a limited range of input values. A local minimum may not be the global minimum.

Lag: The number of periods that price or moving average trails the original data.

Layer: A grouping of slabs (a slab is a group of neurons) in a network. There may be a single slab in a layer or multiple slabs in the same layer. There is only one input layer and one output layer in a network. There may be multiple hidden layers.

Learning Rate: During the learning process, each time a pattern is presented to the network, the weights leading to an output node are modified slightly in the direction required to produce a smaller error the next time the same pattern is presented. The amount of weight modification is the learning rate times the error.

Moving Average Convergence/Divergence (MACD): Is calculated by subtracting a 12-day moving average from a 26-day moving average. A 9-day moving average of the difference is plotted on top of the difference line and acts as a trigger when the two moving averages cross.

Momentum: 1. The momentum of a security is the ratio of a price some days ago to today's price.

2. Large learning rates often lead to oscillation of weight changes and learning never completes, or the model converges to a solution that is not optimum. One way to allow faster learning without oscillation is to make the weight change a function of the previous weight change to provide a smoothing effect. The momentum factor determines the proportion of the last weight change that is added into the new weight change.

Moving Average (MA): A method of calculating the average value of a security's price over a period of time. It is calculated by adding the current value plus $(n - 1)$ previous values divided by n. As the price of the security changes over time, the moving average moves up and down. An MA(5) would indicate a 5-period moving average. Moving averages are usually of a security's price, but can also be applied to indicators such as the RSI.

Neural Network: An artificial intelligence problem solving computer program that learns through a training process of trial and error.

Neuron: 1. The basic building block of the brain, a cell, whose inputs come from the 5 senses.

2. A software imitation of the brain's neuron whose inputs are numbers.

Output: The value or values the network is trying to predict, or the classification values if the network is classifying patterns.

Pattern: A single record (or row) of variables that influence a network's predictions or classifications. A pattern consists of inputs and outputs.

Recurrent Network: Where some of input layer, hidden layer, or output layer is feedback to an additional layer. These networks have the ability to remember patterns; therefore, they are excellent for time series data.

Relative Strength Index (RSI): An index which measures a security's internal strength as measured against itself. When two securities are compared to each other, it is called Comparative Relative Strength.

R-Square: The coefficient of multiple determination, a statistical indicator usually applied to multiple regression analysis. It compares the accuracy of the model to the accuracy of a trivial benchmark model wherein the prediction is simply the mean of all the samples. Perfect predictions result in an R squared of 1. Poor fits result in values near 0.

SPX: Symbol for the S&P 500 Cash Index.

SPY: Symbol for the S&P 500 Futures Index.

Stochastic: An oscillator which compares a security's trading range over the last n-periods to the present price.

Tick: Running total of the number of up trades minus the number of the down trades.

Time Horizon: The period forward for which the a time series forecast is made.

Time Series: A data stream which represents the value of something at regular points in time. Daily stock market prices would be an example.

Training: Training is the process by which the weights inside a neural network are adjusted so that the network can produce the right output(s) for a given set of inputs. Training is also referred to as "learning."

Training Pattern: A data pattern consisting of input variables (and correct output variables for supervised networks) used to train the network.

TRIN: Also known as ARMS Index. Tells whether the stock gaining in price, or those declining in price are getting the greater share of market activity.

YXY: Symbol for the Dow Jones 100 (NYSE) Index.

BIBLIOGRAPHY

Abramowitz, Milton, and Stegun, Irene A., (Eds.), *Handbook of Mathematical Functions,* New York: Dover Publications, 1972.

Adler, P. A., and Adler, P., *The Social Dynamics of Financial Markets,* Greenwich, CT: JAI Press, 1984.

Anderson, James A., and Rosenfeld, Edward, (Eds.), *Neurocomputing,* Cambridge, MA: MIT Press, 1987.

Anderson, James A., Pellionisz, Andras, and Rosenfeld, Edward, (Eds.), *Neurocomputing 2,* Cambridge, MA: MIT Press, 1990.

Anderson, Philip W., Arrow, Kenneth, and Pines, David, (Eds.), The Economy as an Evolving Complex System, *Sante Fe Institute Proc. Vol. V.* Redwood City, CA: Addison-Wesley, 1988.

Ariel, Robert A., High Stock Returns before Holidays: Existence and Evidence on Possible Causes, *J. of Finance, Vol. XLV,* No. 5. pp. 1611–1626, Dec. 1990.

Azoff, E. M., Neural Network Principal Components Preprocessing and Diffraction Tomography, *Neural Computing and Applications, Vol. 1,* pp. 107–114, 1993.

Azoff, E. M., Reducing Error in Neural Network Time Series Forecasting, *Neural Computing and Applications, Vol. 1,* pp. 240–247, 1993.

Babcock, Bruce, Jr., *The Dow Jones-Irwin Guide to Trading Systems,* Homewood, IL: Dow Jones-Irwin, 1989.

Bailey, T. J., *The Elements of Stochastic Processes with Applications to the Natural Sciences,* New York: John Wiley, 1964.

Balsara, Nauzer J., *Money Management Strategies for Future Traders,* New York: John Wiley, 1992.

Band, R. E., *Contrary Investing,* New York: Viking Penguin, 1986.

Battiti, Roberto, First- and Second-Order Methods for Learning, Between Steepest Descent and Newton's Method, *Neural Computation, Vol. 4,* pp. 141–166, 1992.

Battley, Nick, *An Introduction to Commodity Futures and Options,* London: McGraw-Hill, 1989.

Bergerson, Karl, and Wunsch, Donald C., A Commodity Trading Model Based on a Neural Network-Expert System Hybrid, *Proc. IJCNN* Seattle 1991, Vol. 1, pp. 289–293, Piscataway, NJ: IEEE, 1991.

Bloomfield, Peter, *Fourier Analysis of Time Series,* New York: John Wiley, 1976.

Blum, Adam, *Neural Networks in C++,* New York: John Wiley, 1992.

Boashash, Boualem, Estimating and Interpreting the Instantaneous Frequency of a Signal-Part 1: Fundamentals, *Proceedings of the IEEE, Vol. 80,* No. 4, pp. 520–538, April 1992.

Boashash, Boualem, Estimating and Interpreting the Instantaneous Frequency of a Signal-Part 2: Algorithms and Applications, *Proceedings of the IEEE, Vol. 80,* No. 4, pp. 540–568, April 1992.

Bourlard, H., and Kamp, Y., Autoassociation by Multilayer Perceptrons and Singular Value Decomposition, *Biological Cybernetics, Vol. 59,* pp. 291–294, 1988.

Brock, William, Lakonishok, Josef, and LeBaron, Blake, Simple Technical Trading Rules and the Stochastic Properties of Stock Returns. Social Systems Research Institute Workshop Series No. 9022, October 1990. University of Wisconsin-Madison, WI.

Brock, William A., Causality, Chaos, Explanation and Prediction in Economics and Finance. In *Beyond Belief: Randomness, Prediction and Explanation in Science.* ch. 10, John L. Casti and Anders Karlqvist, (Eds.), Boca Raton, FL: CRC Press, 1991.

Brock, William A., Hsieh, David A., and LeBaron, Blake, *A Test for Nonlinear Dynamics,* Cambridge, MA: MIT Press, 1990.

Burke, Gibbons, The Computerised Trader, *Futures, Vol. XXI,* p. 74 May and p. 68, July 1992.

Burke, Gibbons, Perils, Pitfalls and Stumbling Blocks, *Futures, Vol. XXII,* No. 3, pp. 30–34, March 1993.

Burrascano, P., *IEEE Transactions on Neural Networks,* Learning Vector Quantization for the Probabilistic Neural Network. July 1991, 2, pp. 458–461.

Burton, Robert M., Jr., and Mpitos, George J., Event-Dependent Control of Noise Enhances Learning in Neural Networks, *Neural Networks, Vol. 5,* pp. 627–637, 1992.

Callen, Earl, and Shapero, Don, A Theory of Social Imitation, *Physics Today,* pp. 23–28, July 1974.

Casdagli, Martin, Nonlinear Prediction of Chaotic Time Series, *Physica D, Vol. 35,* pp. 335–356, 1989.

Casdagli, Martin, and Eubank, Stephen, (Eds.), *Nonlinear Modeling and Forecasting,* Sante Fe Institute Proceedings, Vol. XII, Redwood City, CA: Addison-Wesley, 1992.

Casti, John L., *Searching for Certainty,* New York: Morrow, 1991.

Caudill, M., and Butler, C., *Naturally Intelligent Systems,* Cambridge, MA: MIT Press, 1990.

Caudill, M., and Butler, C., *Understanding Neural Networks: Computer Explorations, Vols. 1 and 2,* Cambridge, MA: MIT Press, 1992.

Caudill, M., *Neural Networks Primer,* San Francisco, CA: Miller Freeman Publications, 1989.

Chakraborty, Kanad, et al., Forecasting the Behaviour of Multivariate Time Series Using Neural Networks, *Neural Networks, Vol. 5,* pp. 961–970, 1992.

Chen, J. R., and Mars, P., Stepsize Variation Methods for Accelerating the Backpropagation Algorithm, *Proc. IJCNN Washington 1990, Vol. 1,* pp. 601–604, New York: IEEE, 1990.

Chen, Ping, Empherical and Theoretical Evidence of Economic Chaos, *System Dynamics Review 4,* pp. 81–108, 1988.

Chen, S., Cowan, C. F. N., and Grant, P. M., Orthogonal Least Squares Learning Algorithm for Radial Basis Function Networks, *IEEE Transactions on Neural Networks, Vol. 2,* No. 2, pp. 302–309, March 1991.

Cootner, P., (Ed.), *The Random Character of Stock Market Prices,* Cambridge, MA: MIT Press, 1964.

DARPA *Neural Network Study,* Lexington, MA: MIT Lincoln Laboratory, 1988.

Dayhoff, Judith, *Neural Network Architectures: An Introduction,* New York: Van Nostrand Reinhold, 1990.

Dimson, E., (Ed.), *Stock Market Anomalies,* Cambridge: Cambridge University Press, 1988.

Douglas, Mark, *The Disciplined Trader,* New York: NYIF, 1990.

Dreman, David M., *The New Contarian Investment Strategy,* New York: Random House, 1982.

Duda, R., and Hart, P., *Pattern Classification and Scene Analysis,* 2nd ed., New York: John Wiley, 1993.

Dwyer, G. P., and Hafer, R. W., (Eds.), *The Stock Market: Bubbles, Volatility and Chaos,* Lancaster: Kluwer Academic, 1989.

Eberhart, Russell C., and Dobbins, Roy W., (Eds.), *Neural Network PC Tools,* London: Academic Press, 1990.

Efron, B., *The Jackknife, the Bootstrap and Other Resampling Plans,* Philadelphia: SIAM, 1982.

Elman, J. L., Finding Structure in Time, *Cognitive Science, Vol. 14,* pp. 179–211, 1980.

Elman, J. L., and Zipser, David, Learning the Hidden Structure of Speech, *Journal of the Acoustical Society of America, Vol. 83,* pp. 1615–1626, 1988.

Elton, E., and Gruber, M., *Modern Portfolio Theory and Investment Analysis,* 4th ed., New York: John Wiley, 1991.

Epstein, Richard A., *The Theory of Gambling and Statistical Logic,* Rev. ed., New York: Academic Press, 1977.

Farmer, J. Doyne, and Sidorowich, John J., Predicting Chaotic Time Series, *Physical Review Letters, Vol. 59,* pp. 845–848, 24 August 1987.

Feller, William, *An Introduction to Probability Theory and its Applications,* 3rd ed., New York: John Wiley, 1986.

Fishman, Mark B., Barr, Dean S., and Loick, Walter J., Using Neural Nets in Market Analysis, *Technical Analysis of Stocks and Commodities, Vol. 9,* No. 4, p. 18, April 1991.

Fishman, Mark B., and Barr, Dean S., A Hybrid System for Market Timing, *Technical Analysis of Stocks and Commodities, Vol. 9,* No. 8, p. 26, August 1991.

Freedman, Roy S., AI on Wall Street, *IEEE Expert,* pp. 3–9, April 1991.

Gabr, M. M., and Rao, T. Subba, The Estimation and Prediction of Subset Bilinear Time Series Models with Applications, *Time Series Analysis, Vol. 2,* pp. 155–171, 1981.

Goonatilake, Susan, and Treleaven, Philip, (Eds.), *Intelligent Systems for Finance and Business,* Chichester: John Wiley, (in press).

Greising, David, and Morse, Laurie, *Brokers, Bagmen, & Moles,* New York: John Wiley, 1991.

Grossberg, S., *Studies of the Mind and Brain,* Drodrecht, Holland: Reidel Press, 1982.

Hadady, R. E., Finberg, I. L., and Rahfeldt, D., *Winning with the Insiders,* West Palm Beach, FL: Weiss Research, 1987.

Hammerstrom, Dan, Working with Neural Networks, *IEEE Spectrum,* pp. 43–45, July 1993.

Haugen, Robert A., and Lakonishok, Josef, *The Incredible January Effect,* Homewood, IL: Dow Jones-Irwin, 1989.

Hawley, D. D., Johnson, J. D., and Raina, D., Artificial Neural Systems: A New tool for Financial Decision-Making, *Finan. Analy. J.,* p. 63, Nov/Dec 1990.

Haykin, S., *Adaptive Filter Theory,* 2nd ed., Englewood Cliffs, NJ: Prentice-Hall, 1991.

Hebb, D. O., *The Organization of Behavior,* New York: Wiley, 1949.

Hecht-Neilsen, R., *Neurocomputing,* Menlo Park, CA: Addison-Wesley, 1990.

Henon, M., A Two-Dimensional Map with a Strange Attractor, *Communications in Mathematical Physics, Vol. 50,* p. 69, 1970.

Hertz, John, Krogh, Anders, and Palmer, Richard G., *Introduction to the Theory of Neural Computation,* Lecture Notes Volume 1, Sante Fe Institute. Redwood City, CA: Addison-Wesley, 1991.

Hirsch, Yale, *Don't Sell Stocks on Mondays,* New York: Facts on File Publications, 1986.

Hlawatsch, Franz, and Bordreaux-Bartels, G. Faye, Linear and Quadratic Time-Frequency Signal Representations, *IEEE Signal Processing Magazine, Vol. 9,* No. 2, pp. 21–67, April 1992.

Howrey, E. Philip, A Spectrum Analysis of the Long-Swing Hypothesis, *Intrnl. Economic Review, Vol. 9,* pp. 228–252, 1968.

Hsieh, David A., Testing for Nonlinear Dependence in Daily Foreign Exchange Rates, *Journal of Business, Vol. 62,* pp. 339–369, 1989.

Hull, John, *Options, Futures, and other Derivative Securities,* 2nd ed., Englewood Cliffs, NJ: Prentice-Hall, 1993.

Hush, Don R., and Horne, Bill G., Progress in Supervised Neural Networks, *IEEE Signal Processing Magazine, Vol. 10,* No. 1, pp. 8–39, January 1993.

Hutton, L., *Johns Hopkins Applied Physics Lab Technical Digest, Vol. 13,* No. 1, Using Statistics to Assess the Performance of Neural Network Classifiers, 1992.

Johnson, M., *The Random Walk and Beyond,* New York: John Wiley, 1988.

Jolliffe, I. T., *Principal Component Analysis,* Berlin: Springer-Verlag, 1986.

Jurik, Mark, The Care and Feeding of a Neural Network, *Futures, Vol. XXI,* No. 12, pp. 40–44, October 1992.

Jurik, Mark, Consumer's Guide to Neural Network Software, *Futures, Vol. XXII,* No. 8, pp. 36–42, July 1993.

Karlin, S., and Taylor, H. M., *A first Course in Stochastic Processes,* 2nd ed., New York: Academic Press, 1975.

Katz, Jeffrey Owen, Developing Neural Network Forecasters for Trading, *Technical Analysis of Stocks and Commodities, Vol. 10,* No. 4, p. 58, April 1992.

Kaufman, Perry J., *The New Commodity Trading Systems and Methods,* New York: John Wiley, 1987.

Kean, John, Using Neural Nets for Intermarket Analysis. *Technical Analysis of Stocks and Commodities, Vol. 10,* No. 11, p. 58, November 1992.

Kelly, J. L., A New Interpretation of Information Rate, *Bell System Technical Journal, Vol. 35,* pp. 917–926, 1956.

Kendall, Maurice, and J. Keith Ord, *Time Series,* 3rd ed., Edward Arnold, Sevenoaks, Kent, 1993.

Kindelberger, C. P., *Manias, Panics and Crashes,* New York: Basic Books, 1978.

Klimasaukas, Casey, Neural Nets and Noise Filtering, *Dr Dobb's Journal,* pp. 32–48, January 1989.

Knight, Sheldon, Tips, Tricks and Tactics for Developing Trading Systems, *Futures, Vol. XXII,* No. 1, pp. 38–40, January 1993.

Koeckelenberger, Andre, Sunspot Index Data Center, 3 Avenue Circulaire, -1180, Bruxelles, Belgium.

Kohonen, T., *Self Organization and Associative Memory,* 2nd ed., Berlin: Springer-Verlag, 1987; 3rd ed., 1989.

Kolb, Robert W., *Options: The Investor's Complete Toolkit,* New York: New York Institute of Finance, 1991.

Kolmogorov, A., *Foundations of the Theory of Probability,* Trans. N. Morrison, New York: Chelsea, 1956.

Korenberg, Michael J., and Paarmann, Larry D., Orthogonal Approaches to Time Series Analysis and System Identification, *IEEE Signal Processing Magazine, Vol. 8,* No. 3, pp. 29–43, July 1991.

Kosko, Bart, *Neural Networks and Fuzzy Systems,* Englewood Cliffs, NJ: Prentice-Hall, 1992.

Kurkova, Vera, Kolmogorov's Theorem Is Relevent, *Neural Computation, Vol. 3,* pp. 617–622, 1991.

Lashonishok, Josef, and Maberly, Edwin, The Weekend Effect: Trading Patterns of Individual and Institutional Investors, *J.Finance, Vol. XLV,* No. 1, pp. 231–243, March 1990.

Lang, K., and Whitbrock, M., *Proceedings of the 1988 Connectionist Models Summer School,* Learning to Tell Two Spirals Apart.

Lapedes, Alan, and Farber, Robert, Nonlinear Signal Processing Using Neural Networks, Prediction and System Modelling. Los Alamos Report LA-UR-87-2662, Los Alamos National Laboratory, Los Alamos, NM, 1987.

Larrain, Maurice, Testing Chaos and Nonlinearities in T-Bill Rates, *Financial Analysts Journal, Vol. 47,* No. 5, pp. 51–62, Sep/Oct 1991.

Le Cun, Yann, Une Procedure d'Apprentissage pour Reseau a Seuil Assymetrique, *In Cognitiva 85: A la Frontiere de Intelligence Artificielle des Sciences de la Connaissance des Neurosciences,* CESTA, Paris, pp. 599–604, 1985.

Le Cunn, Yann, Denker, John S., and Solla, Sara A., Optimal Brain Damage, *Advances in Neural Information Processing Systems 2,* pp. 598–605, Ed. D. S. Touretzky. San Mateo, CA: Morgan Kaufmann, 1990.

Li, J., Michel, A. N., and Porod, W., *IEEE Transactions on Circuits and Systems, Vol. 36,* No. 11, pp. 1405–1422. Analysis and synthesis of a class of neural networks: linear systems operating on a closed hypercube, November, 1989.

Lippman, R. P., *IEEE ASSP Magazine,* pp. 4–22, An Introduction to Computing with Neural Nets, April 1987.

Lorenz, H. W., *Nonlinear Dynamical Economics and Chaotic Motion,* Lecture Notes In Economics and Mathematical Systems No. 334, Berlin: Springer Verlag, 1989.

Luenberger, D. G., *Introduction to Linear & Nonlinear Programming,* Reading, MA: Addison-Wesley, 1973.

Lutzy, Ottmar, and Dengel, Andreas, A Comparison of Neural Net Simulators, *IEEE Expert,* pp. 43–51, August 1993.

Mackay, C., *Extordinary Popular Delusions and Madness of Crowds,* New York: Noonday Press, 1974 (Rep. of 19th century ed.).

Maren, Alianna, Harston, Craig, and Pap, Robert, *Handbook of Neural Computing Applications,* London: Academic Press, 1990.

Marowitz, Harry, *Portfolio Selection: Efficent Diversification of Investments,* New York: John Wiley, 1964.

Marple, S. Lawrence, Jr., *Digital Spectral Analysis,* Englewood Cliffs, NJ: Prentice-Hall, 1987.

Masters, Timmothy, *Practical Neural Network Recipes in C++,* Orlando, FL: Academic Press, 1993.

Mathews, V. John, Adaptive Polynomial Filters, *IEEE Signal Processing Magazine, Vol. 8,* No. 3, pp. 10–26, July 1991.

McClelland, James L., and Rumelhart, David E., and the PDP Research Group, Parallel Distributed Processing, Vol. 2: Psychological and Biological Models. Cambridge, MA: MIT Press, 1986.

McClelland, James L., and Rumelhart, David E., *Explorations in Parallel Distributed Processing,* Cambridge, MA: MIT Press, 1988.

McClish, D. K., Comparing the Areas Under More than Two Independent ROC Curves, *Medical Decision Making, Vol. 7,* pp. 149–155, 1987.

McCulloch, W. S., and Pitts, W. H., *Bulletin of Mathematical Biophysics,* A logical calculus of ideas immanent in nervous activity, Vol. 5, pp. 115–133, 1943.

McQueen, G., and Thorley, S., Are Stock Returns Predictable? A test using Markov Chains, *J Finance, Vol. XLVI,* No. 1, p. 239, March 1990.

Mead, W. C., et al., Prediction of Chaotic Time Series using CNLS-NET-Example: The Mackey-Glass equation, *Nonlinear Modeling and Forecasting,* pp. 39–72.

Miller, R. M., *Computer-Aided Financial Analysis,* Reading, MA: Addison-Wesley, 1990.

Miller, W. T., Sutton, R. S., and Werbos, P., *Neural Networks for Robotics and Control,* Cambridge, MA: MIT Press, 1990.

Minsky, Marvin L., and Papert, Seymour A., *Perceptrons,* Expanded Edition. Cambridge, MA: MIT Press, 1988.

Muller, Berndt, and Reinhardt, Joachim, *Neural Networks: An Introduction,* New York: Springer-Verlag, 1990.

Murphy, John J., *Technical Analysis of Futures Markets,* New York: New York Institute of Finance, 1986.

Newbold, Paul, *Statistics for Business and Economics,* 2nd ed., Englewood Cliffs, NJ: Prentice-Hall, 1988.

Nguyen, D., and Widrow, B., *International Joint Conference of Neural Networks,* The truck backer-upper: an example of self-learning in neural networks, Vol. 2, pp. 357–363, July 1989.

Nguyen, D., and Widrow, B., *International Joint Conference of Neural Networks,* Improving the learning speed of 2-layer neural networks by choosing initial values of the adaptive weights, Vol. 3, pp. 21–26, July 1990.

Nishikawa, Y., Kita, H., and Kawamura, A., *Proceedings of the International Joint Conference on Neural Networks,* NN/I: A Neural Network Which Divides and Learns Environments, I-684 to I-687, January 1990.

NYIF, *Futures: A Personal Seminar,* New York: New York Institute of Finance, 1989.

O'Reilly, Brian, Computers That Think Like People, *Fortune,* pp. 58–61, 27 Feb 1989.

Orfanidis, Sophocles J., Gram-Schmidt Neural Nets, *Neural Computation, Vol. 2,* pp. 116–126, 1990.

Owens, A. J., and Filkin, D. L., Efficient Training of the Backpropagation Network by Solving a Stiff Ordinary Differential Equations, *Proc IJCNN,* Washington 1989, Vol. 2, pp. 381–386, New York: IEEE, 1989.

Pardo, Robert, *Design, Testing and Optimisation of Trading Systems,* New York: John Wiley, 1992.

Parker, D. B., LE Learning Logic, Technical Report TR-47, Center for Computational Research in Economics and Management Science, Cambridge, MA: MIT Press, 1985.

Pau, L. F., Artificial Intelligence and Financial Services, *IEEE Trans. Knowledge and Data Engineering, Vol. 3,* pp. 137–148, 1991.

Peters, Edgar E., *Chaos and Order in the Capital Markets,* New York: John Wiley, 1991.

Poulos, E. Michael, Futures According to Trend Tendency, *Technical Analysis of Stocks and Commodities, Vol. 10,* No. 1, p. 61, January 1992.

Press, William H., Teukolsky, Saul A., Vetterling, William T., and Flannery, Brian P., *Numerical Recipes,* 2nd ed., Cambridge, MA: Cambridge University Press, 1992.

Priestley, Maurice B., *Spectral Analysis and Time Series,* London: Academic, 1981.

Priestley, Maurice B., *Nonlinear and Nonstationary Time Series Analysis,* London: Academic, 1988.

Refenes, A. N., et al., Currency Exchange Rate Prediction and Neural Network Design Strategies, *Neural Computing & Applications, Vol. 1,* pp. 46–58, 1993.

Resinkoff, H. L., Foundations of Arithmeticum Analysis: Compactly Supported Wavelets and the Wavelet Group, Aware Report

AD890507.1, 1989. Aware, Inc, One Memorial Drive, Cambridge, MA.

Rioul, Oliver, and Vetterli, Martin, Wavelets and Signal Processing, *IEEE Signal Processing Magazine, Vol. 8,* No. 4, pp. 14–38, October 1991.

Rissanen, J., *Stochiastic Complexity in Statistical Inquiry,* Singapore: World Scientific, 1989.

Rosenblatt, F., *Principles of Neurodynamics,* Washington, DC: Sparten Press, 1961.

Ruelle, David, Deterministic Chaos, the Science and the Fiction, *Proc Royal Soc London A, Vol. 427,* pp. 241–248, 1990.

Rumelhart, D. E., Hinton, G. E., and Williams, R. J., Learning Representations by Backpropagating Errors, *Nature, Vol. 323,* pp. 533–536, 1986.

Rumelhart, D. E., Hinton, G. E., and Williams, R. J., *Parallel Data Processing,* Learning internal representations by error propagation, Vol. 1, Chapter 8, pp. 318–362, Cambridge, MA: MIT Press, 1986.

Rumelhart, D., and McClelland, J., *Parallel Distributed Processing,* Cambridge, MA: MIT Press, 1986.

Rutterford, Janette, *Introduction to Stock Exchange Investment,* London: Macmillan, 1985.

Savit, Robert, Nonlinearities and Chaotic Effects in Options Prices, *J Futures Markets, Vol. 9,* pp. 507–518, 1989.

Savit, Robert, Chaos on the Trading Floor, *New Scientist,* p. 48, 11 August 1990.

Schiller, Robert J., *Market Volatility,* Cambridge, MA: MIT Press, 1989.

Schmerken, I., Wall Street's Elusive Goal, Computers that Think Like Pros, *Wall Street Computer Review, Vol. 7,* pp. 61–69, June 1990.

Schwager, Jack D., *A Complete Guide to the Futures Markets,* New York: John Wiley, 1984.

Schwager, Jack D., Selecting the Best Futures Price Series for Computer Testing, *Technical Analysis of Stocks and Commodities, Vol. 10,* No. 10, pp. 65–71, October 1992.

Schetzen, M., *The Voltera and Weiner Theory of Nonlinear Systems,* New York: John Wiley, 1980.

Shanno, David F., Conjugate Gradient Methods with Inexact Searches, *Mathematics of Operations Research, Vol. 3,* pp. 244–256, 1978.

Shanno, D. F., and Kang-Hoh, Phua, Matrix Conditioning and Nonlinear Optimisation, *Mathematical Programming, Vol. 14,* pp. 149–160, 1978.

Shih, Yin Lung, Neural Nets in Technical Analysis, *Technical Analysis of Stocks and Commodities, Vol. 9,* No. 2, p. 62, February 1991.

Simpson, P., *Artificial Neural Systems,* New York: Pergamon Press, 1990.

Siu, Sammy, and Cowan, Colin F. N., Adaptive Equalization Using the Back Propagation Algorithim, *Proc. Second Intl Artificial Neural Networks Conference,* Bournemouth, 1991, pp. 10–12. London: IEE, 1991.

Sluis, A. van der, and Vorst, H. A. van der, The Rate of Convergence of Conjugate Gradients, *Numerical Mathematics, Vol. 48,* pp. 543–560, 1986.

Specht, D., *Proceedings of the IEEE International Conference on Neural Networks,* Probabilistic Neural Networks for Classification, Mapping, or Associative Memory, 1, pp. 525–532, 1988.

Specht, D., *Neural Networks,* Probabilistic Neural Networks, 3, pp. 109–118, 1990.

Specht, D., and Shapiro, P., *Proceedings of the International Joint Conference on Neural Networks,* Generalization Accuracy of Probabilistic Neural Networks Compared with Back-Propagation Networks, July 8 12, 1, pp. 887–892, 1991.

Specht, D., *IEEE Transactions on Neural Networks,* A General Regression Neural Network, 2, 6, pp. 568–576, Nov. 1991.

Stockbro, Kurt, and Umberger, D. K., Forecasting with Weighted Maps, *Nonlinear Modeling Forecasting,* pp. 73–94.

Sugihara, George, and May, Robert, Nonlinear Forecasting as a way of Distinguishing Chaos from Measurement Error in Time Series, *Nature, Vol. 344,* pp. 734–741, 19 April 1990.

Swales, George S., Jr., and Yoon, Young, Applying Artifical Neural Networks to Investment Analysis, *Financial Analysts Journal, Vol. 48,* No. 5, Sep/Oct 1992.

Takens, F., Detecting Strange Attractor in Turbulence, *Lecture Notes in Mathematics,* D. Rand and L. Young (Eds.), Berlin: Springer, 1981.

Taylor, S. J., *Modeling Financial Time Series,* Chichester: John Wiley, 1986, reprinted 1994.

Teweles, R. J., and Jones, F. J., *The Futures Game*, 2nd ed., New York: McGraw-Hill, 1987.

Thompson, J. M. T., and Stewart, H. B., *Nonlinear Dynamics and Chaos*, Chichester: John Wiley, 1986.

Thorp, Edward O., *The Mathematics of Gambling*, Van Nuys, CA: Gambling Times Press, 1984.

Thorp, Edward O., and Kassouf, Sheen T., *Beat the Market: A Scientific Stock Market System*, New York: Random House, 1967.

Tong, Howell, *Nonlinear Time Series: A Dynamical System Approach*, Oxford: Oxford University Press, 1990.

Tong, Howell, and Lim, K. S., Threshold Autoregression, Limit Cycles and Cyclical Data, *J Royal Statistical Society, Vol. B 42*, pp. 245–292, 1980.

Touretzky, D., and Pomerleau, D., *What's Hidden in the Hidden Layers*, Byte 14, pp. 227–233, 1989.

Vaga, Tonis, The Coherent Market Hypothesis, *Financial Analysts Journal, Vol. 46*, No. 6, pp. 36–49, Nov/Dec 1990.

Vince, Ralph, *Portfolio Management Formulas*, New York: John Wiley, 1990.

Vince, Ralph, *The Mathematics of Money Management*, New York: John Wiley, 1992.

Vogel, T. P., Mangis, J. K., Rigler, A. K., Zink, W. T., and Alkon, D. L., *Biological Cybernetics*, Accelerating the convergence of the back-propagation method, Vol. 59, pp. 257–263, 1988.

Wallich, Paul, Wavelet Theory: An Analysis Technique that's Creating Ripples, *Scientific American*, pp. 34–35, January 1991.

Wasserman, P., *Neural Computing. Theory and Practice*, New York: Van Nostrand Reinhold, 1989.

Weigend, Andreas S., Huberman, Bernardo A., and Rumelhart, David E., Generalisation by Weight-Elimination with Application to Forecasting, *Advances in Neural Information Processing Systems 3*, pp. 875–882. Richard P. Lippmann, John E. Moody, and David S. Touretzky, (Eds.), San Mateo, CA: Morgan Kaufmann, 1991.

Weigend, Andreas S., Huberman, Bernardo A., and Rumelhart, David E., Predicting Sunspots and Exchange Rates with Connectionist Networks, *Nonlinear Modeling and Forecasting*, pp. 395–432.

Weigand, Andreas S., Huberman, Bernardo A., and Rumelhart, David E., Backpropagation, Weight-Elimination and Time Series Prediction, *Connectionist Models, Proceedings of the 1990 Summer*

School. D. S. Touretzky, et al., (Eds.), San Mateo, CA: Morgan Kaufmann, 1991.

Weiss, Sholom M., and Kulikowski, Casimer A., *Computer Systems That Learn,* San Mateo, CA: Morgan Kaufmann, 1991.

Werbos, P., Beyond Regression: New Tools for Prediction and Analysis in the Behavioral Sciences, PhD Thesis, Harvard University, 1974.

White, H., Economic Prediction Using Neural Networks, The Case of IBM Daily Stock Returns, *Proc. IEEE Int Conf on Neural Networks, Vol. 2,* pp. 451–458, New York: IEEE, 1988.

Widrow, B., and Sterns, S. D., *Adaptive Signal Processing,* New York: Prentice-Hall, 1985.

Wong, F. S., et al., Fuzzy Neural Systems for Stock Selection, *Financial Analysts Journal, Vol. 48,* No. 1, pp. 47–52, Jan/Feb 1992.

Zaremba, Thomas, Technology in Search of a Buck, Chapter 12 in *Neural Network PC Tools.*

Ziemba, William T., A Better Simulation: The Mathematics of Gambling, *Gambling Times,* June 1987.

INDEX